Athletic Forever

THE KERLAN-JOBE ORTHOPAEDIC CLINIC PLAN FOR LIFETIME FITNESS

Frank Jobe, M.D., Neal ElAttrache, M.D.,
and Karen Mohr, P.T., S.C.S., with T. G. Rand

Forewords by Magic Johnson and Tommy Lasorda

CB
CONTEMPORARY BOOKS

Library of Congress Cataloging-in-Publication Data

Jobe, Frank W.
    Athletic forever : the Kerlan-Jobe orthopaedic clinic plan for
lifetime fitness / Frank Jobe, Neal ElAttrache, and Karen Mohr with
T. G. Rand; forewords by Magic Johnson and Tommy Lasorda.
       p.   cm.
     ISBN 0-8092-2863-7
    1. Sports injuries—Prevention—Popular works.   2. Physical
fitness—Popular works.   I. ElAttrache, Neal.   II. Rand, T. G.
III. Title.
RD97.J63   1998
617.1'027—dc21   98-8345
                                           CIP

Interior design by Monica Baziuk
Interior production by Hespenheide Design
Interior illustrations and stretching chart by Morri Mohr
Interior photographs courtesy of Centinela Hospital Medical Center, unless
otherwise indicated

Published by Contemporary Books
A division of NTC/Contemporary Publishing Group, Inc.
4255 West Touhy Avenue, Lincolnwood (Chicago), Illinois 60646-1975 U.S.A.
Printed in the United States of America
International Standard Book Number: 0-8092-2863-7
99 00 01 02 03 04 LB 19 18 17 16 15 14 13 12 11 10 9 8 7 6 5 4 3 2 1

Contents

PART 1 Lifetime Fitness

PART 2 The Kerlan-Jobe Injury Guide

PART 3 The Kerlan-Jobe Athlete's Resource Guide

Foreword by Magic Johnson

Over the span of my athletic career, I have come to realize that athleticism is not just a gift given to you by your parents, but rather a lifetime pursuit. As a kid and as a young athlete, sports were a way for me to have fun. The added benefit from being out there on the basketball court was that I became fit. As time went on, it became apparent to me that fitness is not something to be taken for granted. Now, I need to work at maintaining my health and fitness in order to avoid injury and to enjoy life.

Participation in sports inevitably leads to injury at some point, because an athlete is constantly pushing himself to the edge to improve. While on the edge, he walks a fine line between peak performance and impending injury. The physicians of the Kerlan-Jobe Orthopaedic Clinic represent the cutting edge in the science and technology of sports medicine. They have spent years helping thousands of elite athletes get in and stay in top shape. They have also helped professional athletes overcome injuries, both minor and career threatening, so that they can continue doing what they love to do most—compete. In this book, the authors share with you their recommendations for designing a safe and effective fitness program. This program, based on scientific information, will not only help you achieve your individual goals, but will help you do so while avoiding injury.

The information the authors include in this book is a conglomeration of years of experience treating athletes and expert scientific knowledge. They have assembled all the information you will need to get fit and stay fit throughout your life. This book will help you to understand the balance of components that make up a good fitness program, including cardiovascular training, strength training, and stretching exercises. Achieving that balance will allow you to stay in shape and enable you to continue the sports and activities you enjoy. Maintaining fitness and health is a goal to actively pursue throughout your life, and *Athletic Forever* can make that goal a reality.

Foreword by Tommy Lasorda

As long as I have known the authors, they have devoted their lives to taking care of and fine-tuning the bodies of a broad spectrum of athletes, from the weekend warriors to the elite professionals. They have written this book for those who want to know how to take care of their bodies as the years pass—and for those who want to understand the science behind how their body works, the changes their body will undergo with time, and how to use fitness to affect those changes in a positive way.

The goals of any singular fitness program can be as varied as the number of individuals participating in those programs. Furthermore each individual's fitness goals may change a number of times throughout life. The health benefits, such as weight loss and lowered blood pressure, that can be achieved through a fitness program and proper nutrition are of utmost importance to me. For others, a sub-three-hour marathon or a 100-mile bike ride might be the ultimate achievement. This book will not only help you to meet your goals, but it will help you understand the science behind how you got there and how to best avoid injury on the way there.

Having experienced sports as a professional athlete, a coach, and a manager, I have learned that the best treatment for injury is prevention. However, it is inevitable that anyone who challenges his or her body will face injury at some point. Nothing is more frustrating to an athlete than closing in on his or her goals only to be sidelined by an injury. The elite team of sports-medicine physicians at the Kerlan-Jobe Orthopaedic Clinic have compiled years of wisdom they have gained by treating the world's best athletes and put it into an easy-to-follow injury guide. This guide will help all athletes understand why injuries occur, what they can do to help themselves, and when they need to seek professional evaluation and treatment.

As I have discovered through my personal-health struggles, fitness is not something to be taken for granted—rather it is a lifelong process in which you need to take a proactive role. This book takes the reader leaps and bounds beyond a recipe for fitness. It bridges the gap between science and practice to help athletes of all levels achieve their ever-changing goals to be the best they can be.

Acknowledgments

T. G. Rand wishes to acknowledge the patience, perseverance, and guidance of Matthew Carnicelli and Kristen Eberhard at NTC/Contemporary Publishing.

Special thanks as well to Clive Brewster of HealthSouth. Further gratitude is owed to the researchers at the exercise physiology laboratory of the University of Southern California, Dr. Alan Abbott for sharing his valuable information on the Massai people, Paul King for helping to initiate this project, and Karen Mohr of the Kerlan-Jobe Orthopaedic Clinic for her painstaking work in ensuring the accuracy of the information contained herein.

Finally, I'd like to thank James G. Hornfischer of the Literary Group for his constant support and hard work on my behalf.

Introduction

There's an old joke—an ancient one, probably—about the man who goes to his doctor, bends his arm at the elbow, and says, "Doc, it hurts when I do this." The doctor replies, "Then don't do that."

That, in a nutshell, was what constituted the field of sports medicine 25 years ago. Athletes were plagued by injuries that we used to call *career-enders*—ruptured rotator cuffs, torn knee ligaments, chronic tendinitis. The best advice one could offer was along the lines of, "Stay off it," "Don't use it," or, "Have you considered what you might do after sports?"

Through a combination of skill and good fortune, a new generation of clever and determined physicians such as those here at the Kerlan-Jobe Orthopaedic Clinic have put an end to most career-enders. It seems routine now, but when we developed the procedures and exercises that restored such athletes as Tommy John and Orel Hershiser to peak form, it was generally unheard of for a player to get back in the game after a serious injury (or even a mild one, if it was chronic).

Today's professional athletes play faster, harder, and longer than their predecessors. They bounce back from injury more quickly. Certainly, they look different—just compare the physiques of legendary Olympian Jesse Owens and the modern-day sprinter Michael Johnson. In brief, today's athletes have all kinds of knowledgeable resources to help them maintain levels of fitness and performance that were unknown to their predecessors—very little of which has filtered down to the average individual.

Hence this book. For the first time, a staff of doctors who routinely minister to the world's finest athletes have set down on paper their best prescriptions for health, fitness, and performance. What's that crunching sound in your knee? How soon can you start using a sprained ankle? What can you do to improve or maintain your endurance? What's the best way to maintain a low body fat percentage? It's all here, presented in a way that is designed to help you get in—and stay in—great athletic shape, while avoiding injury.

Lifetime Fitness

1

Age, Conditioning, and Performance

What Happens When You Age?

As physicians who work with athletes every day, we can tell you informally that when a patient understands the "why" about his condition, the "how" and "what" of helping him become much easier to implement. If you want to get straight to the meat of the exercises, Chapter 5 awaits. But if you want to know why your body's performance seems to decline just a little bit with each passing year, stick around—you may find the information presented here motivational, to say the least.

The best way to understand the aging process is to think of your body as an architectural structure. While the building is being built, it doesn't really need to be maintained. Scores of workers are ambulating within the space, welding beams, laying new pipe, fastening joints, and sealing corners. Once they're done, however, and have closed up their tool kits and moved on, the building still needs to be maintained—no matter how well it's constructed.

Your body, for the most part, is under construction until your late teens. A few bones will continue to fuse for several more years, but virtually everything else has been built. Up to that point, anything that tears, strains, or breaks will rapidly heal—the builders, after all, are still "on site." But once they're done, you begin to go through gradual changes:

3

- Bone density diminishes, leading to an increased susceptibility to stress fractures.
- Muscle fibers decline in size and number. In addition, the amount of connective tissue in skeletal muscles increases, so muscles are less pliable.
- *Tendons*, which attach bone to muscle, lose about a fifth of their strength and stretchiness, becoming more prone to tears and ruptures.
- *Collagen fibers*, which are a component of the ligaments and joint capsules that surround and protect joints, become thinner and shorter.
- *Cartilage*, the smooth outer surface that coats bones where they meet at joints, becomes thinner and more brittle.
- Speed and reflexes decline.
- Recovery from exertion takes longer.
- *Metabolism*—the amount of calories your body burns to sustain itself—decreases, so you tend to accumulate more fat. Overall muscle mass decreases. A body that has more fat is less efficient at burning calories than a lean, muscular body, so a sort of vicious cycle is set up (one that we'll tell you how to beat).
- There is a marked decrease in the function of your cardiovascular system. By the time a man reaches his 40s, his *arteries*—the delicate pathways carrying blood from the heart—become occluded (narrowed) by about 33 percent. (The damage actually begins happening much earlier; autopsies of young men reveal that the fatty streaks that are precursors of coronary artery disease begin as early as the teen years). As a result of decreased circulation to the tissues of the body, healing takes place at a slower rate.
- There is a natural rise in blood pressure as you age. More serious problems arise, including cardiovascular disease—some form of which (hypertension, stroke, and heart attack among them) now afflicts one in four Americans.
- The amount of blood pumped by the heart—*cardiac output*—decreases.
- Aerobic capacity, an important measure of athletic performance, diminishes by about 9 percent each decade.
- Your ability to take in and process oxygen through the lungs decreases because of a reduction in elasticity of the membranes and air cells of the lung.

- Vision deteriorates as a result of macular degeneration, cataracts, glaucoma, and other conditions.

KJ FACT: Middling Pains

The majority of sports-related injuries strike people between the ages of 21 and 55, the so-called middle years.

Chronological Age Versus Biological Age

Are these changes inevitable? It was once thought so. Athletic fitness was believed to be a gift, one that didn't require much cultivation. It would burn brightly while an individual was in the teens and 20s and then dissipate. Athletes who outlasted their colleagues chronologically were thought to be curiosities, but for the most part their physical conditioning deteriorated rapidly along with their age.

A range of new scientific disciplines has all but destroyed that mindset. Exercise physiology, biomechanics, rehabilitation therapy, and sports medicine are just a few of the areas that have experienced rapid growth in the past two decades, demonstrating that even though the body ages, it never loses its adaptive capacity—its ability to meet the demands of athletic performance—if those demands continue to be applied in a measured and thoughtful fashion.

That's why we've begun to differentiate between a man's chronological, or calendar age, and his biological age. Your driver's license may indicate that you're twice the legal age for voting, but if your heart, lungs, and muscles are accustomed to vigorous activity, then biologically, you may be much younger.

Aging affects people to such varying degrees that it's no longer easy to say who is young and who is old. In the course of a day here at the Kerlan-Jobe Orthopaedic Clinic, it's not uncommon for us to see 60-year-old men who have the metabolism, body fat, and aerobic capacity of men half their age. But we also see 30-year-old men who are obese, easily winded, and show signs of heart disease.

At the exercise physiology lab of the University of Southern California, where Kerlan-Jobe doctors serve as physicians to the college's athletic teams,

Dr. Robert Wiswell and his staff have been conducting long-term studies of older athletes between the ages of 40 and 90 who defy the conventional thinking about aging. Many of them have body fat percentages and aerobic capacities of college students.

At one time, this sort of subversion of findings would have been, as we said, a curiosity, attributable purely to an individual's genetic legacy. But a mounting body of evidence demonstrates convincingly that when it comes to the aging process, genes, which you can't control, are only one determinant. A second one, which you can control, is the quality and quantity of the physical activity you engage in.

Among the more impressive studies that first pointed the way to this line of thinking:

- In the 1950s, researchers in England studied postal workers and bus company employees, two groups that include work forces evenly divided between physically active employees (bus conductors and mail carriers) and inactive employees (drivers and counter clerks). Researchers found that the workers who worked on their feet had half the risk of heart attack of those who worked sitting down.
- Scientists studying native cultures—the Massai tribe of Kenya and the Pima Indians of northern Mexico in particular—have been impressed by the virtual absence of heart disease and diabetes among these active tribespeople. Yet in both cases, those members who leave their communities and move to westernized cities experience skyrocketing rates of heart disease, diabetes, and obesity. Among Pimas who move to the towns and cities of Arizona, the incidence of obesity and diabetes is an astonishing 54 percent. Clearly, the genetic propensity for heart disease exists among these groups, but their traditional, active lifestyles seem to play a role in keeping those individuals biologically young.
- In the 1970s, researchers studied dockworkers in San Francisco and found that those who had the most physically demanding jobs—the cargo handlers—had the lowest incidence of cardiovascular disease. In addition, cargo handlers who were promoted to desk and supervisory jobs lost their *cardioprotectiveness* and became more susceptible to heart disease. In other words, their cardiovascular systems were granted a sort

of immunity against the decay that normally accompanies the aging process. This indicated, again, that it wasn't genes, but a lack of physical activity that predisposed them to serious illness.

As a result of studies like these, we've come to understand that many of the diseases and conditions once thought to be the result of aging are, quite the contrary, the result of inactivity. They come not from being old, but from acting old.

The General Adaptation Syndrome

Why is this so? Going back to our architectural structure, imagine that a building has a built-in system that causes it to be only as sturdy as it needs to be. In mild, sunny weather, its walls are thin and permeable, its windows only loosely sealed, and its beams weak and insubstantial. But in blustery, wintry weather, it becomes sturdier, tighter, and more dependable.

That's how your body is designed—to adapt to whatever degree of stress is placed on it. This process is known as the *general adaptation syndrome*. It explains how your body senses extra demands that are placed on it, then adapts to become stronger so that those demands no longer threaten its state of equilibrium. Because of this phenomenon, targeted strength conditioning (which we discuss later in this book) builds muscle. It can't replace lost muscle fiber, but it can thicken and strengthen what you've got. Studies have shown that even men in their 60s, 70s, and 80s can double their muscular strength in just 12 weeks through a series of simple conditioning exercises.

The ability to adapt was once an important survival mechanism that allowed people to conserve or expend energy depending on such things as environment and food availability. Today, physical survival is no longer a useful regulator. And in a society where you can go from dawn till dusk without needing to expend much physical energy at all, the body adapts by going into virtual sleep mode. Muscles become thinner and bones become brittle. These effects are known as *hypokineticism,* and they occur because of lack of movement.

The effects of hypokineticism occur rapidly. Three months of forced immobility, such as what you might go through if you had a fractured limb placed in a cast, leads to a temporary condition called *osteoporosis of disuse* and results in a 30 percent reduction in bone density when compared to the non-cast limb.

Fortunately, your body adapts to use as well as disuse; in fact, it thrives on movement. When you exercise properly, your bones become denser, your joints become more fluid, your muscles become stronger, and your heart pumps blood more efficiently—at any age.

KJ FACT: All Heart

An active 50-year-old man has an aerobic capacity that is as much as 30 percent higher than that of a sedentary man half his age.

Adaptive Changes in the Cardiovascular System

Nowhere are the changes caused by exercise (or the lack of it) more important than in your cardiovascular system. *Aerobic capacity*, or *$\dot{V}O_2max$* (which stands for maximum volume of oxygen), may be the most important of ten *biomarkers*, physiological factors that were identified by government researchers as being indicators of your body's biological age (as opposed to its chronological age). As a rule, $\dot{V}O_2max$ is thought to decline by about 9 percent per decade of life, in large part due to the stiffening and weakening of your heart muscle. But we now know that with a program of consistent, targeted exercise, you can reduce that number to less than 5 percent per decade. We even suspect that athletes who continue to remain vigorously active may experience no loss at all in their aerobic capacity, even through the age of 60. Aerobically, they can run, bike, and sprint with the energy of a college student.

The cardiovascular system adapts to exercise by "growing younger," even among people who suffer from cardiovascular disease. A dramatic study at Case Western University (performed on animals) proved that when a damaged heart (one with blocked arteries that limit the flow of blood) is

KJ CLOSEUP: Biomarkers

Ten biomarkers were identified by researchers as being indicators of physiologic function:

1. *Muscle mass:* The size and number of muscle fibers decrease by 30 percent between ages 20 and 70. You lose about seven pounds of muscle mass per decade after young adulthood.

2. *Strength:* Closely tied to muscle mass, strength and speed of muscle contractions diminish as one ages.

3. *Basal metabolic rate:* The amount of energy required to sustain bodily processes at rest decreases by about 2 percent each decade. As a result, the average adult will burn 100 less calories a day each decade.

4. *Body fat percentage:* The amount of fat in relation to total body weight increases as a result of metabolic changes and decreasing muscle mass. Between a man's mid-20s and his mid-60s, the percentage of body fat nearly doubles. High body fat percentage is closely associated with risks for heart disease and early death.

5. *Aerobic capacity:* The ability to use oxygen for fuel at a high level of functioning declines by about 9 percent per decade.

6. *Blood sugar tolerance:* Fat requires more *insulin* (a hormone responsible for lowering blood sugar levels) to regulate blood sugar, which is why about one-third of adults may develop adult-onset diabetes by the time they reach age 70.

7. *Cholesterol ratio:* Fatty plaques formed by cholesterol increase with age, a fact that is often indicated by a change in blood cholesterol levels.

8. *Blood pressure:* There is a steady increase in blood pressure during each decade of life.

9. *Bone density:* Age-related osteoporosis can decrease bone mass and bone density by as much as 50 percent by the time an individual reaches his 60s.

10. *Thermoregulation:* The body loses its ability to regulate its internal temperature, which affects the efficiency of your cardiovascular system.

exercised, the body builds new pathways of blood vessels to circumvent the diseased area so that blood flow increases. These *collateral vessels*, as they are known, help restore the heart's oxygen supply.

Meanwhile, the healthy heart grows stronger, too. Researchers at the Baylor College of Medicine have shown that the heart's capacity for growing and adapting to exercise continues even until a man's 80s. Many of the Masters athletes participating in studies at the University of Southern California didn't even begin a program of physical activity until well into their 50s and 60s, yet their gains have been remarkable.

KJ FACT: No Speeding at 70?

Between ages 20 and 70, the average man loses 30 percent of muscle cells, or about seven pounds of muscle, per decade. That translates into a loss of speed and strength. Targeted conditioning can prevent or reverse that loss of muscle.

Other Adaptive Changes

To summarize, here are the physiological factors influenced positively by physical activity:

- *Heart:* Exercise increases cardiac capacity, so your heart pumps more blood per minute. Your resting heart rate decreases, allowing your heart to work more efficiently. Your heart recovers more quickly after strenuous exertion, allowing for better performance during anaerobic sports such as tennis, sprinting, and soccer.
- *Lungs:* Exercise will help you breathe more efficiently, allowing your lungs to take in and process more oxygen with fewer and deeper breaths. Conditioned athletes can get the same amount of respiratory benefits from six breaths as the average person gets from 20.
- *Blood:* Higher red blood cell count and higher blood volume (increased blood volume is due to both an increase in blood plasma and an increase in red blood cells) translate into more oxygen-carrying ability, better hydration, and improved ability to dissipate heat, and therefore less tendency for the body to become overheated.

- *Aerobic capacity ($\dot{V}O_2$max):* Exercise will cause an increase in $\dot{V}O_2$max, the best measure of athletic fitness. A conditioned individual over 50 has a $\dot{V}O_2$max that is 20 to 30 percent higher than a sedentary man half his age, and 50 percent higher than a same-aged person who is a former athlete but is now inactive.

- *Blood pressure:* Exercise helps decrease both severe and mild *hypertension* (high blood pressure) and is increasingly being prescribed by physicians as a way of helping patients avoid or reduce blood pressure medications, which often have unpleasant side effects.

- *Muscles:* Both *muscular strength* (the ability to move a certain amount of weight or generate force for one powerful movement) and *muscular endurance* (the ability to perform a motion repeatedly for long periods without fatigue such as pumping your legs while cycling or swinging a tennis racket) undergo very little decline among older, active athletes.

- *Connective tissue:* Collagen fibers, one of the components that comprise the connective tissue that forms ligaments, tendons, and the capsule that surrounds joints, can become short and thin with age and disuse. When joints are kept active, the fibers remain thick and strong.

- *Bone density:* Exercise wards off osteoporosis and increases bone density in ways that are specific to the type of exercise or sport you do. Handball players have a higher bone density in the *cervical spine* (the upper portion of the spine) because of the way their heads cock to follow the rapid trajectory of the ball. Rowers have increased bone density in the *lumbar spine* (lower spine), which is involved in pulling the oar through the water.

- *Hormone levels:* Exercise helps inhibit the decline of essential hormones, including the male sex hormone testosterone, and regulates hormones that control sleep patterns.

- *Vision:* A study of elderly male athletes revealed that those who enjoy a lifelong history of aerobic activities have significantly improved vision compared to their inactive counterparts.

- *Reflexes:* Exercise improves response time; older active men have quicker responses than younger inactive men in their early 20s.

Maladaptation and Overtraining

There can be a downside to the general adaptation syndrome, though. Just as detrimental to your body as inactivity is activity that is beyond what your muscles and joints are ready to bear. Technically, this phenomenon is known as *maladaptation*. You could also call it the *weekend warrior syndrome*, or any other name—but it's a certain recipe for injury. Sometimes the injury occurs suddenly—a tendon ruptures, a hamstring strains. Other times, the injury can be more insidious, building slowly until inflammation sets in and becomes chronic and unyielding causing those dreaded "itises"—tendinitis, bursitis, and so on—that linger for long periods.

In either case, such occurrences are far less random than you might think. If the trigger that sets your body into a mode of adaptation is too great, you won't adapt. Your body will make an effort to meet the demands placed upon it, but it will become exhausted before it can meet those demands. The very system that is activated in an effort to build muscles and bones will shut down from overload.

The word *overtraining* refers to a more systemic form of maladaptation. It describes a level of fatigue that doesn't diminish within an hour after your workout. If the word *overtraining* has any glamour to it, it shouldn't; overtraining syndrome has derailed many athletes, both professional and recreational. It's even been associated with *chronic fatigue syndrome*, a condition that can leave you feeling listless and debilitated for weeks or even months. Yet overtraining syndrome is not difficult to spot. One of the symptoms is that your workout leaves you feeling fatigued rather than energized. Some fatigue is normal for up to about an hour after you've finished exercising; but if you're still tired several hours later, you may be overtraining.

Other symptoms that can arise due to overtraining include increased susceptibility to colds and flus, mood disturbances, irritability, appetite changes, and even sleep problems. What's important to remember is that your body's tissues don't grow during exercise; to the contrary, they break down. The growth phase that allows you to become stronger and more fit comes with adequate rest and recovery.

The key to avoiding overtraining, therefore, is adequate rest and recovery between periods of exercise and vigorous sports. In general, a muscle that has been stressed but not injured can recover within 48 to 72 hours, so follow a hard workout with a day or two of light activity (known as *active rest*). In addition, make gains slowly. If you want to increase speed, distance, the amount of weight you lift, the number of tennis sets you play—build gradually. If you make athleticism a lifetime pursuit, then you'll have a lifetime to improve.

2

Fit, Fat, Healthy: How Do You Rate?

Now that you have a general idea of how aging and exercise can affect your health, performance, and body appearance, it's time to get personal—specifically, to assess your current level of health and fitness. Blood pressure, body fat percentage, heart rate, and cholesterol levels are among the barometers we're going to use. They'll give you an idea of not only how healthy you are at this very moment, but also where you fall in terms of your risk for heart disease and premature death.

In a previous era, you might have lived your life without knowing these measurements. Even if you had known them, you probably wouldn't have known what you could do to improve them. That's all changed dramatically in the last few years. Today, you can check your blood pressure in a kiosk at many local pharmacies; you can screen your cholesterol levels at home (though we don't recommend it because the information provided is limited compared with what you can learn from a similar screening at the doctor's office); and you can have your body fat percentage tested at your local health club.

As for benefiting from such information, we now know based on recent studies that diet and exercise can not only reduce your risk factors for heart disease, they can *reverse* them. Exercise lowers blood pressure, and it increases high-density lipoproteins, or HDL (colloquially referred to as "the good cholesterol," because increased levels of HDL have been shown to have a protective effect on the cardiovascular system). Diet can lower the "bad cholesterol"—low-density lipoproteins, or LDL, high amounts of which are associated with increased risk for heart disease.

Even though you can do many of these tests on your own, we strongly recommend having them done under the supervision of your physician. Only a medical professional can do a thorough job of interpreting how each of these findings relate individually to you.

KJ FACT: A One-Two Health Punch

Exercise can help increase your percentage of HDL, or good cholesterol. A healthy, lowfat diet can reduce your percentage of LDL, or bad cholesterol.

Tests for Cardiovascular Health

Test: Electrocardiogram (also known as ECG or EKG)

Purpose:

Uncovers serious abnormalities in the rhythm and function of your heart.

Description:

The exam is painless and takes a few seconds. Twelve small discs are taped to your chest while an electronic needle scratches out a graphic recording of electrical changes during heart activity. A typical ECG consists of a series of three characteristic wave patterns. In a normally functioning heart, the size, duration, and timing of the wave patterns is consistent. Changes in the pattern or timing of the ECG recording may signal a diseased or damaged heart or indicate that the heart is having problems conducting the electrical signals that lead it to contract and pump blood.

What you should know:

In some cases, it may be advisable or necessary to undergo a stress ECG, which involves a physician observing how your heart functions while you exert yourself, either running on a treadmill or pedaling on an exercise bike. A chart displays your heart pattern and blood pressure during various stages of your workout and will give the physician information about how your heart functions under stress.

Test: Blood pressure

Purpose:

Blood pressure readings tell you how much force is being exerted against the walls of your arteries as blood travels through them; the higher the pressure, the harder your heart has to work. A blood pressure measurement consists of two numbers: the *systolic pressure* (the top number) and the *diastolic pressure* (the bottom number). The systolic pressure is the peak pressure in the blood vessels when your heart is contracting; the diastolic pressure is the pressure in the blood vessels when the heart is in a relaxed state. Chronic high blood pressure, or *hypertension*, will, over a period of years, take its toll by causing tears and cracks in the delicate blood vessels.

Description:

Electronic blood pressure monitors or inflatable cuffs are used. The healthcare professional listens for the pulses in your arm that indicate the systolic and diastolic readings. The preferred blood pressure reading is a maximum of 120/80—that means that during a contraction of your heart muscle, your blood is exerting enough pressure to send the mercury inside a calibrated gauge shooting up to 120 millimeters, and up to 80 millimeters when the heart is between contractions. Readings higher than 140/90 are considered mildly or moderately high; readings over 180/105 are considered severely high.

What you should know:

The cause of hypertension, in the majority of cases, is unknown, though heredity plays an important role. Modifying your lifestyle with exercise, a nutritious lowfat diet, and the elimination of alcohol and tobacco use can help reduce both moderate and severe hypertension. If you have severe hypertension, your doctor will probably opt to lower it with medication before allowing you to embark or continue on an exercise program.

Test: Cholesterol levels

Purpose:

Determines how much cholesterol is circulating in your bloodstream. Cholesterol can accumulate along the walls of your arteries, narrowing the blood vessels and making

KJ TIP: Mistaken Case of Hypertension

It's common for people without hypertension to experience a harmless and temporary spike when having their blood pressure measured in a doctor's office. The phenomenon is caused by simple anxiety and is known as *white coat hypertension*. It leads to misdiagnosis in about one-fifth of all cases. If your blood pressure measures high the first time, it should be taken a second time, 10 to 15 minutes later, after you've had a chance to relax. Sit comfortably with your uncuffed arm hanging loosely at your side while the healthcare professional takes the reading.

it more difficult for your heart to pump blood out to the body. Left unchecked, it causes a condition known as *atherosclerosis* (hardening of the arteries), which can eventually lead to heart failure if one of the vessels that brings blood to the heart muscle itself is affected.

A total cholesterol screening will measure:

- Low-density lipoproteins, or LDL (the "bad cholesterol"). These high-fat molecules are the form of cholesterol most associated with atherosclerosis. The higher the number, the greater your risk for heart disease.
- High-density lipoproteins, or HDL (the "good cholesterol"). These molecules are high in protein and low in fat. They circulate through the bloodstream, collecting fattier types of cholesterol for removal from the body. A high HDL count can help prevent heart disease.
- Triglyceride levels. Triglycerides are used for energy, but excess amounts saturate the blood and can also contribute to arterial disease.

The type of cholesterol screening done at a health fair or your local health club can only give you information about total cholesterol. It cannot give you information about the breakdown of the types of cholesterol in your blood.

Cholesterol measurements are interpreted as follows:

Total Cholesterol

Preferred: . . . . 160 to 200 mg/dl (milligrams per deciliter of blood)
(the lower the better)
Borderline high: . . . . 200 to 239 mg/dl
High: . . . . 240 mg/dl and over

HDL

Preferred: . . . . Greater than 45 mg/dl

Low: . . . . Less than 35 mg/dl

LDL

Preferred: . . . . 130 mg/dl or lower

Borderline high: . . . . 130 to 159 mg/dl

High:. . . . . 160 mg/dl or higher

Triglycerides

Preferred: . . . . Less than 200 mg/dl

Borderline high: . . . . 200 to 400 mg/dl

High:. . . . . 400 to 1,000 mg/dl

Very high: . . . . Greater than 1,000 mg/dl

Description:

Blood is drawn from your arm, and a small vial of the blood is sent to a laboratory. Results are available within a few days. In order for the test to be effective, you should abstain from eating for at least nine hours prior to the test (thus this test is often referred to as *fasting cholesterol*). It's best to schedule the test for early in the day.

What you should know:

In one study, men who had average cholesterol levels of 260 (well into the high range) were able to reduce them to under 200 in just eight months by engaging in a program that combined a lowfat diet with consistent aerobic exercise.

A measurement that is increasingly used is the *cholesterol ratio*, which describes the ratio between total cholesterol and HDL. The lower the ratio, the lower the risk for heart disease. For example, an endurance athlete who monitors his diet by eating lowfat foods—and so has the benefit of controlling his cholesterol levels on two fronts, exercise and diet—might have a total cholesterol of 160, with an HDL level of 64; that yields an excellent ratio of 2.5:1. On the other hand, a sedentary person already suffering from heart disease might have a ratio as high as 6:1.

If you have high cholesterol, a reasonable target to aim for is 4:1—a total level of 190 to 200, with an HDL of 45 to 50. If you suffer *familial hypercholesteremia*—in other words, if you have a genetic predisposition to high cholesterol—then exercise and diet alone may not improve your profile. In such cases, your physician might prescribe a cholesterol-lowering drug.

KJ QUIZ: Should You See a Doctor First?

The following questionnaire was developed by the National Institutes of Health and is designed to identify whether you need clearance from a physician before beginning or continuing an exercise program. (The questionnaire is called the PAR-Q, or Physical Activity Readiness Questionnaire, after a similar quiz developed by Canadian fitness researchers.)

Physical Activity Readiness
Questionnaire - PAR-Q
(revised 1994)

PAR - Q & YOU

(A Questionnaire for People Aged 15 to 69)

Regular physical activity is fun and healthy, and increasingly more people are starting to become more active every day. Being more active is very safe for most people. However, some people should check with their doctor before they start becoming much more physically active.

If you are planning to become much more physically active than you are now, start by answering the seven questions in the box below. If you are between the ages of 15 and 69, the PAR-Q will tell you if you should check with your doctor before you start. If you are over 69 years of age, and you are not used to being very active, check with your doctor.

Common sense is your best guide when you answer these questions. Please read the questions carefully and answer each one honestly: check YES or NO.

YES	NO		
☐	☐	1.	Has your doctor ever said that you have a heart condition <u>and</u> that you should only do physical activity recommended by a doctor?
☐	☐	2.	Do you feel pain in your chest when you do physical activity?
☐	☐	3.	In the past month, have you had chest pain when you were not doing physical activity?
☐	☐	4.	Do you lose your balance because of dizziness or do you ever lose consciousness?
☐	☐	5.	Do you have a bone or joint problem that could be made worse by a change in your physical activity?
☐	☐	6.	Is your doctor currently prescribing drugs (for example, water pills) for your blood pressure or heart condition?
☐	☐	7.	Do you know of <u>any other reason</u> why you should not do physical activity?

If

you

answered

YES to one or more questions

Talk with your doctor by phone or in person BEFORE you start becoming much more physically active or BEFORE you have a fitness appraisal. Tell your doctor about the PAR-Q and which questions you answered YES.

• You may be able to do any activity you want—as long as you start slowly and build up gradually. Or, you may need to restrict your activities to those which are safe for you. Talk with your doctor about the kinds of activities you wish to participate in and follow his/her advice.

• Find out which community programs are safe and helpful for you.

NO to all questions

If you answered NO honestly to <u>all</u> PAR-Q questions, you can be reasonably sure that you can:

• start becoming much more physically active—begin slowly and build up gradually. This is the safest and easiest way to go.

• take part in a fitness appraisal—this is an excellent way to determine your basic fitness so that you can plan the best way for you to live actively.

DELAY BECOMING MUCH MORE ACTIVE:

• if you are not feeling well because of a temporary illness such as a cold or a fever — wait until you feel better; or

• if you are or may be pregnant — talk to your doctor before you start becoming more active.

Please note: If your health changes so that you then answer YES to any of the above questions, tell your fitness or health professional. Ask whether you should change your physical activity plan.

<u>Informed Use of the PAR-Q</u>: The Canadian Society for Exercise Physiology, Health Canada, and their agents assume no liability for persons who undertake physical activity, and if in doubt after completing this questionnaire, consult your doctor prior to physical activity.

Reprinted from the 1994 revised version of the Physical Activity Readiness Questionnaire (PAR-Q & You). The PAR-Q & You is a copyrighted, pre-exercise screen owned by the Canadian Society for Exercise Physiology.

Tests for Body Fat Composition

Test: Body fat composition

Purpose:

Body fat composition testing tells you what percentage of your overall body weight consists of lean skeletal muscle and bone and what percentage is extra baggage—fat. An individual's percentage of body fat is correlated not only with fitness level but also with increased susceptibility to heart disease, diabetes, and early mortality.

Description:

The two most common methods for determining body fat are *hydrostatic weighing* and *skinfold testing*.

Hydrostatic weighing, the more accurate but less widely available method, is based upon the principle that different substances that occupy the same volume or amount of space on dry land will displace different amounts of water when they are submerged, because of their density. Since fat has a different density than muscle, the hydrostatic weight of two people who are the same height, weight, and build will be different depending upon their percentages of fat and lean tissue. Hydrostatic weighing is favored by many professional sports organizations and research facilities.

The more accessible method of measuring body fat is skinfold measurements. A gauge (called a *caliper*) is used to gently pinch a fold of skin. The amount of fat you have just beneath the skin in various parts of the body—such as the triceps, abdomen, and back—is calculated and factored into a formula that determines the amount of overall fat in your body.

Skinfold calipers are sold for anywhere from $10 to $50, but despite the detailed instructions they come with, they're only useful in the hands of an experienced fitness professional. Check with your local YMCA or health club to have the test performed properly.

What you should know:

Some body fat is essential for maintaining cellular and organ health. The lowest acceptable range is about 3 to 5 percent for men, and 8 to 12 percent for women. Few people have body fat anywhere near that low level, but men should ideally keep their body fat down below 20 percent, and women should top out at no higher than 30 percent. Once the figures climb beyond those percentages, there is increased susceptibility to a wide range of problems, including shortness of breath, hypertension, lowered resistance to infection, adult-onset diabetes, and cardiovascular disease.

Test: Body mass index (BMI)

Purpose:

Offers a quick, general impression of one's probable body fat percentage using a simple arithmetic formula. Although it doesn't distinguish between body fat and lean muscle mass, the BMI, which is used by insurance underwriters, can also point to risk factors for illness or early death.

Description:

To determine your BMI:

a. Multiply your weight by 703.
b. Calculate the square of your height in inches (for example, if you're six feet tall, then $72 \times 72 = 5,184$).
c. Divide "a" by "b."

What you should know:

A BMI of approximately 20 to 27 puts you in the low risk range; greater than a 30 indicates a heightened risk for cardiovascular disease.

Tests for Aerobic Fitness

Test: The one-mile walking test

Purpose:

A simple way to determine how efficiently your body uses oxygen.

Description:

On a closed high school or college track, walk as fast as you can for one mile, then measure yourself against the following chart:

Excellent	Less than 10:12 minutes
Good/High	10:13–11:42 minutes
Average	11:43–13:13 minutes
Low/Average	13:14–14:44 minutes
Fair	14:45–16:23 minutes
Poor	More than 16:24 minutes

What you should know:

If you're in good health, you can do this test alone; put in your best effort in order to get the truest results. Precede the test with a 10- to 20-minute warm-up and follow with a 5-minute cool-down.

KJ CLOSEUP: Five Numbers to Watch

1. *Body fat percentage:* A strong indicator of both health and fitness levels. Keep it down by combining calorie control with exercise.

2. *Cholesterol:* Most serum cholesterol comes from dietary fat, in particular the saturated fats found mostly in animal products. (Dietary cholesterol is a very small contributor to cholesterol, so don't be fooled by foods that advertise themselves as being cholesterol-free—it's the fat content you need to watch.) To increase HDL, do aerobic exercise for at least 20 minutes, three times a week.

3. *Blood pressure:* Contributing factors to hypertension include emotional stress, family history of the disease, lack of physical activity, and poor diet. Exercise can help control mild, moderate, and severe hypertension. Severe cases may require medication as well, but lifestyle modifications can reduce the amount of medicine you have to take.

4. *Resting heart rate:* Normal range is 60 to 100 beats per minute. An exercise program should lower your rate within two weeks—a sign that your heart's working more efficiently.

5. *Caloric intake:* The U.S. government suggests that an individual's average caloric intake should range between 2,000 and 2,500 calories. However, your true proper daily caloric intake is a highly individual measurement that is a product of your weight, gender, level of fitness, body fat percentage, and the intensity of your daily physical activities. If desired, make an appointment with a nutritionist to assess your true dietary needs.

Test: Morning heart pulse (resting heart rate)

Purpose:

To determine your *resting heart rate*, the number of times your heart beats at complete rest. The figure is used in finding your target heart rate and is also a relative measure of aerobic fitness—generally speaking, the lower your resting heart rate, the more efficiently your heart is working. (Note: a low heart rate that is not associated with fitness, a condition known as *bradycardia*, may require medical attention.)

Description:

Do the test within five minutes of waking. If your bladder is full, empty it, as a full bladder may cause a higher reading. Then recline or sit comfortably in a chair. Lightly touching the pulse in your wrist (the *radial pulse*) or your neck (the *carotid pulse*), measure your heart rate for exactly 60 seconds. Write the figure down. Perform the test five days in a row and average the numbers together.

What you should know:

True resting heart rate (abbreviated as RHR) is more accurately called morning resting pulse, since mornings are when you get the most accurate readings. The average population has an RHR range of about 60 to 100 beats per minute. Among endurance athletes, it can be as low as 35 beats per minute (lower in rare cases; also rare is a much higher rate among some elite athletes). Generally speaking, you may experience a fitness-related decline in heart rate by 5 to 10 beats per minute if you engage in frequent cardiovascular exercise and aerobic sports.

KJ TIP: Resting Pulse

Monitoring your resting pulse can help you avoid overtraining. If your resting pulse rises over several days, it is often a sign that you've either been training too hard or are coming down with a cold or flu. In either case, ease up on your exercise, or take a day off.

Once you've established your RHR, monitor it periodically to gauge your progress. An increase above your normal average can indicate that you're overtraining.

Test: Age-estimated maximum heart rate (MHR)

Purpose:

Used in determining your proper target heart range for aerobic exercise, your MHR is the fastest number of times your heart will beat under intense exertion.

Description:

There are two simple, commonly used formulas:

- *Method 1*   If you haven't exercised for a long time, use this method: subtract your age from 220 (the average high-end heart rate of a newborn infant) to arrive at an estimate of your MHR. For example, if you are 40 years old, your age-estimated MHR is 220 − 40, or 180.

- *Method 2*   If you're in good cardiovascular shape, use this method: divide your age by 2 and subtract that number from 205. It will yield a slightly higher number than the first method. That means that when you're setting your target heart range for some of the exercises discussed in Chapter 5, you'll be working at a slightly higher level of intensity.

Test: $\dot{V}O_2$max (maximum aerobic capacity)

Purpose:

To determine the point during exercise at which $\dot{V}O_2$max, or maximal oxygen consumption, occurs. This is the most accurate measurement of aerobic fitness.

Description:

The test requires the use of a breathing valve for collection and analysis of expired air during an exercise test that is usually performed running on a treadmill. $\dot{V}O_2$max is determined by analyzing the exhaled air to determine the point at which oxygen uptake by the body fails to increase with an increased workload. As this test requires technologically advanced and expensive equipment, it is not widely available. For a healthy individual, exercise guidelines can be established by using a predicted maximum heart rate rather than $\dot{V}O_2$max.

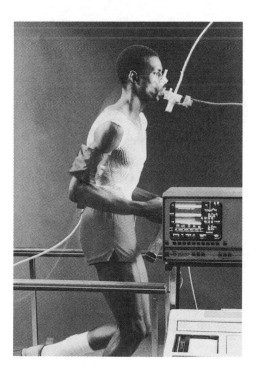

A special air-collection system is used to precisely measure aerobic capacity.

3

Your Body as Machine

What makes you tick, run, perform? It's a combination of matter and ether: the strength of your muscles and bones, the resiliency of your heart, and the interplay of brain and body via a series of electrical signals. Let's take a look under the hood at the components required to build and maintain an athletic body.

Cardiovascular System

Your athletic potential begins inside the four chambers responsible for moving oxygen and nutrients throughout your body. The heart, about the size of a fist, is actually two pumps: the two right chambers exchange blood with the lungs, where the blood is infused with oxygen, while the left chambers funnel blood to your muscles. The circulating blood performs another crucial activity: after it drops off the fuel, it carts away waste products like lactic acid and carbon dioxide, biological "pollutants" that are created when your muscles burn fuel.

At rest, your heart circulates only about five liters of blood per minute, whatever your level of fitness. Very little of that goes toward supplying the skeletal muscles, the ones you need for movement. However, during intense physical activity, your muscles can siphon off as much as 90 percent of all the blood that's circulating in your body. Your heart responds by pumping out greater volumes of blood, as much as 40 liters of blood per minute in an elite athlete.

If the muscles can't get enough oxygen from the blood, they go after other energy sources like *glycogen*, a muscle fuel made from the carbohydrates you take in through your diet. Burning glycogen doesn't occur in significant amounts unless you either are exercising very intensely or are so out of shape that any activity makes you gasp for air. Because glycogen depletes rapidly, it's not an ideal fuel source for endurance activities—while oxygen is. The more efficiently you use oxygen, the better you'll perform. That's why oxygen is considered the gold standard of athletic fitness. It's measured by a figure we mentioned earlier known as $\dot{V}O_2$max, or maximum aerobic capacity, and it defines the limits of the hardest work you're able to achieve using oxygen for fuel.

KJ FACT: You Can Increase Your $\dot{V}O_2$max with Exercise

When you begin to follow a targeted, progressive exercise program, you'll achieve what experts call the *training effect*. Your aerobic capacity improves because:

- *Stroke volume*, the amount of blood pumped per beat, increases.

- *Cardiac output*, the amount of blood pumped each minute, increases.

- *Heart rate*, the number of times the heart beats each minute, decreases. That means the heart works less hard while moving more blood.

What Is Aerobic Activity?

Any exercise that causes your heart and lungs to work hard enough to improve your capacity for producing muscular energy is an aerobic exercise. Any activity can be aerobic if it's done long enough and at the right intensity. Generally, the most effective exercises for aerobic improvements are those that involve a rhythmic, continuous movement of the large muscle groups. In the gym, that would mean the treadmill, exercise bike, or stairclimber. There are also plenty of outdoor sports such as cross-country skiing, speed skating, running, cycling, rowing, and swimming that are excellent aerobic exercises.

KJ FACT: Fuel Systems

Your muscles draw energy from one of three metabolic systems:

- *ATP-PC (adenosine triphosphate–phosphocreatine):* An anaerobic fuel source that provides immediate, intense power of very short duration. Examples: Jumps, short sprints.

- *Anaerobic glycolysis (lactate system):* Another anaerobic fuel that provides up to approximately three minutes of energy for intense muscular exertion. Examples: Longer sprints such as quarter- and half-miles.

- *Aerobic system:* Uses oxygen to fuel activity that is maintained at a moderate level of intensity. It can continue to provide energy for prolonged periods. Examples: Long jogs, runs, and bike rides.

Fuel Systems

The body uses three different fuel systems to power its muscles during athletic activity, two of which are *anaerobic* (meaning *without oxygen*) and one of which is *aerobic* (*powered by oxygen*). Each sport has its own specific configuration of how these systems are used. The anaerobic systems provide energy quickly for intense bouts of exercise but cannot sustain energy production for extended periods of time. The body uses the aerobic system when energy is needed for exercise that is less intense and longer in duration.

In the 100-meter sprint—which elite athletes run in under 10 seconds, or the equivalent of about 25 miles per hour—the ATP-PC (adenosine triphosphate–phosphocreatine) system is the primary source of energy. This tiny but potent fuel reserve becomes completely depleted in less than eight seconds, and the entire body contains no more than about three ounces of it. In fact, it runs out before the sprint is even over, and for the last 20 meters the athletes run on sheer momentum. Basketball players who sprint down the court, mountain bicyclists who power their bikes over downed logs, and volleyball players who leap for a spike all draw upon the ATP-PC system. Given 30 seconds of recovery, the ATP-PC system can replenish itself for yet another powerful burst if needed.

A second potent anaerobic fuel source, known as the *lactic acid system*, supplies an additional two or three minutes of intense power. Rowers and speed skaters rely on this form of energy. However, it has the unpleasant effect of causing a waste product known as *lactic acid* to build up in the muscles. You may have experienced lactic acid buildup after running uphill or climbing stairs. Your thighs start to burn until eventually your muscles stall out. That's lactic acid leaving its mark.

The third fuel source is the *aerobic system*. Three ingredients go into the efficient use of aerobic energy:

- *Processing:* When you breathe in air, your lungs extract oxygen.
- *Delivery:* Your heart sends unoxygenated blood into the lungs, where the blood picks up oxygen. The oxygenated blood returns to the heart and is then shipped out to the working muscles.
- *Utilization:* The ability of working muscles to absorb all the oxygen being delivered is a function of how well-trained the muscles are. This is usually the limiting factor in how well you are able to perform. If you are a swimmer and your cardiovascular system is in peak condition, running may still leave you winded—that is, until your leg muscles adapt to the requirements of running. Generally speaking, you will use oxygen more efficiently in the exercises you're most accustomed to doing.

KJ CLOSEUP: Atp—A Fuel for All Reasons

No matter which of the three fuel systems your body is using, each is merely a facilitator for resupplying the body with its real source of power—atp, or adenosine triphosphate (so called because it has three phosphate molecules), the muscle fuel. Atp-pc is one of the processes for replenishing atp. It uses phosphocreatine (pc) stored in the muscles to create new atp molecules. When atp separates during muscle contraction, it loses a phosphate molecule. Pc supplies the phosphate molecule for more atp.

When an electrical signal from the brain arrives at the site of a muscle, it triggers the release of calcium, which in turn causes a reaction in atp that sends one of the phosphate molecules flying off on its own and releasing energy in the process. That mini-explosion is what provides the energy for muscle fibers to shorten—they pull together like telescoping rods (*sliding filaments* is the technical term), resulting in the contractions that give you speed, strength, and power. This combustible compound resides right inside the muscle tissue, in tiny manufacturing plants known as *mitochondria*.

But while exercising can increase the size and number of mitochondria (and hence the potential number of ATP molecules) in your body, ATP remains in very short supply and needs to be constantly replenished.

That's where aerobic and anaerobic energy come in. In the ATP-PC system, the PC—which stands for phosphocreatine—restores the missing phosphate molecule. But just like ATP, PC also is in limited supply and runs out in under eight seconds.

The lactic acid system replenishes ATP with a chemical reaction that involves glucose molecules—the stuff derived from your food intake, primarily carbohydrates. Unfortunately, in the lactic acid system, the exchange rate between glucose and ATP is costly—one glucose molecule will get you only two new molecules of ATP, thus limiting your energy span. In addition, there is that lactic acid buildup to contend with.

In the aerobic system, the exchange rate is much better—when you're exercising at an intensity that allows you to process adequate levels of oxygen, you can get 36 ATP molecules for each glucose molecule. The more fit you are, the more intensely you will be able to exercise and still stay in this aerobic zone, even when working at a pace that makes other people gasp to catch up. In fact, that's the whole point of aerobic exercise—to get your fitness up to a point where oxygen is your main currency for manufacturing more ATP.

In case you're wondering what happens to the "missing" phosphate that ATP keeps losing in the mini-explosions, it goes on to become something of a biological renegade. Like other molecules released during chemical reactions in the body, the phosphate becomes a free radical and has the potential to cause cellular damage in the form of oxidation. Because vigorous exercise can increase the number of free radicals circulating in the body, it's particularly important for athletes to eat nutritious foods high in antioxidants, such as cruciferous vegetables.

Let's take a look at the fuel systems in action. When you wake up in the morning and go for a jog, the first systems to provide fuel are the anaerobic ones. That's because it takes several minutes for the aerobic process to kick into gear. Your heart rate needs to reach a point where it is pumping a sufficient amount of oxygenated blood to the muscles, and the capillaries leading to the muscles need to dilate in order to adequately exchange that oxygen with the muscles.

During those first few moments, while you are waiting for your aerobic system to kick in, depending on how hard you run, you'll accumulate some lactic acid that won't be completely cleared out until after you've stopped exercising and your heart rate has returned to its resting rate. Here's important advice for your aerobic exercise routines: a good, slow warm-up will leave you with less lactic acid buildup, and thus you'll be more comfortable and less fatigued throughout the remainder of your workout.

Oxygen Debt

If you've ever wondered why your heart rate doesn't immediately return to its resting rate after you finish exercising, that's because it's repaying a debt that you owe.

When you exercise anaerobically—either at the start of a workout before your aerobic system kicks in, or when increasing the intensity of exercise during a workout—your muscles are working with less oxygen than they need. Due to the good graces of your anaerobic system, the muscles comply, but eventually you have to repay them that oxygen. That happens after you've finished exercising—so your heart takes awhile to calm down because it's still working aerobically to cover that debt.

Now here's the real surprise: if you want to recover quickly following an aerobic workout, you should keep exercising at a very light pace. Since it's the transport of oxygenated blood that repays the oxygen debt and clears lactic acid away from your muscles, exercising at about 30 percent of your $\dot{V}O_2$max (that's a very light jog or a brisk walking pace) will speed your recovery time. So if you're playing multiple sets of tennis, walk around a bit between sets and get that lactic acid out of your system.

The more fit you are, the more rapidly your heart will recover from exertion. If you play a sport that involves fast sprints and charges—such as basketball, tennis, soccer, or football—then it's important to have a good recovery rate. To improve your recovery rate, perform sprint intervals; run hard on a track or treadmill for 30 seconds to two minutes, and then recover for an equal length of time. Sprint intervals should be done for 6 to 10 sets each workout session.

To build short-term sprint power, you need to perform some training at a much higher intensity, above the threshold at which the body's fuel system switches to anaerobic energy. This is known as *anaerobic threshold* (AT) *training*. It works by both increasing your tolerance for lactic acid buildup and by raising the threshold at which your body dips into its anaerobic fuel reserves. Some studies have shown that elite distance runners can function at 90 percent of their aerobic capacity for up to 30 minutes without accumulating lactic acid—that's about 20 percent higher than the range at which most people go anaerobic and nearly run out of energy.

Musculoskeletal System

Bones, cartilage, ligaments, tendons, joint capsules, joints, and muscles are the important components of the musculoskeletal system. Nearly all of these structures are comprised of *connective tissue*, which consists of living cells surrounded by a matrix, or a collection, of fibers suspended in a material called *ground substance*. Each tissue structure is uniquely defined by the type of cell it contains and the type and amount of fibers in its matrix. The combination of strength and flexibility you need to perform well is rooted in the qualities of strength and elasticity provided by your connective tissue.

The two types of fibers contained in connective tissues are *collagen fibers* and *elastic fibers*. Collagen fibers are extremely strong but have very little give to them. Elastic fibers, on the other hand, contain a protein called *elastin* that gives the fibers exceptional resiliency. Bone, ligaments, tendons, joint capsules, and cartilage are each designed to have a balance of collagen and elastic fibers suited to their individual function.

Bone

Bone or *osseous tissue* supports the body and protects vital organs such as the heart and lungs by enclosing them in cagelike structures. Significantly, bone also provides levers for the muscles to act on. Mature bone cells are called *osteocytes*, and they lie within a matrix of mostly collagen fibers (the strong stuff). What gives a bone extra rigidity is the calcium that is stored in its matrix.

There are several types of bones: long bones, such as the leg and arm bones; short bones, found in the hands and feet, which are used as levers to transmit force and for manual handling; flat bones, including the scapula and pelvis, which are broad housings that protect underlying soft tissue in addition to aiding movement; and irregular bones, which are those found in the skull and the spine. Most bones stop growing during adolescence, but some, such as those in the nose and lower jaw, continue to grow throughout life. Bone is, in general, a very vascular tissue, meaning it has an abundant blood supply. This means that under normal conditions, its ability to heal and repair itself is excellent.

Although most bone growth stops by early adulthood, bones are constantly undergoing a "remodeling" process whereby bone reabsorption (bone loss) is balanced by new bone deposition—in other words, bone is always "under construction." It would cost you a fortune to remodel your house on a daily basis, but you can remodel your bones every day by maintaining a sensible conditioning program.

If a bone is constantly exposed to stress, it will step up the remodeling process and respond to that stress by increasing the rate at which it lays down new bone. If bones are exposed to the stress of vigorous exercise, they will increase in density. Rowers, who put great demands on their backs, have been shown to have increased density in the bones of their lower spine.

The increase in bone density in response to stress does not happen instantaneously. Thus, if you exercise too intensely, remodeling cannot keep up with your level of exertion, and a stress fracture may occur. If you continue to train with a stress fracture, it may eventually develop into a full-fledged fracture.

In the presence of inactivity, the remodeling process works in reverse. Lack of stress to the weight-bearing bones of the body can cause bone reabsorption to occur faster than bone deposition, resulting in weak or brittle bones.

KJ FACT: Bone Injuries

Bones fracture either as a result of stress or trauma. Stress fractures begin as tiny cracks along the surface of a bone and can be caused by overtraining. A common site of stress fractures is the *tibia*, or shin bone, in the lower leg; but stress fractures can occur on any bone, even on the body's strongest long bone, the *femur* (thigh bone).

Fractures caused by trauma or impact are either closed (contained beneath the surface of the skin) or open (piercing the skin—also known as a compound fracture) and fall into one of the following categories:

- *Comminuted:* The bone shatters into tiny chips; the trauma is usually very severe.

- *Transverse:* A "clean" break—the result of a direct blow. (Stress fractures that are left unchecked can progress to transverse fractures.)

- *Oblique:* The bone breaks at an angle; the trauma is usually severe.

- *Spiral:* The bone breaks as a result of being twisted, leaving ends that are fractured in a corkscrew pattern.

- *Nondisplaced:* A fracture that causes no obvious deformity; without consulting a physician, you might mistake it for a sprain or contusion. (The old adage that "If you can move it, it's not broken," is wrong, so if a fracture is even slightly suspected, see a doctor.)

- *Avulsion:* A fracture that occurs when bone has been separated from the site where a tendon or ligament attaches. A sudden, jarring impact that stresses the Achilles tendon, for example, can cause the tendon to rupture at the site where it attaches to bone, pulling a chip of bone away from the joint.

Cartilage

Cartilage contains cells called *chondrocytes*, which are embedded in a matrix that is approximately 80 percent water and contains a predominance of collagen fibers. Cartilage has excellent shock absorption properties and functions to resist compressive forces. That's why you're so springy when you're young. However, as you age, the water content of cartilage decreases, causing a corresponding decrease in the ability of the cartilage to absorb shock.

Compounding the problem, cartilage is *avascular*—meaning it doesn't have its own blood supply and therefore does not heal well. So an injury to cartilage, combined with aging, can limit your performance substantially.

There are two important types of cartilage—*hyaline cartilage* and *fibrocartilage*. Hyaline cartilage, also known as *articular cartilage*, is the most abundant type of cartilage in the body. It lines the ends of the bones that come together to form a joint and absorbs shock to protect the bones. When articular cartilage is injured or wears away, as in degenerative arthritis, it can no longer act as a shock absorber, and all the shock is transmitted to the underlying bone.

Fibrocartilage is similar to hyaline cartilage but is slightly more spongy. It is located in areas of the body that need additional shock absorption capability, such as the knee joint and the spine. In the knee, the fibrocartilage, or *meniscus*, acts as an extra shock absorber to protect the articular cartilage, which protects the underlying bone. When you hear someone refer to "torn cartilage" in the knee, they are referring to a tear in the meniscus. Because the meniscus, like other cartilage, is avascular, it gets its nutrition from nearby blood supplies serving the adjacent bone.

While its regenerative capacity is low, cartilage does have some adaptive ability. When you work out, the cells in the cartilage increase in size, making the cartilage thicker and stronger. Even a simple 10-minute warm-up will cause cartilage to swell with protective fluids by as much as 13 percent, which is just one of the reasons why you should always ease into an exercise session slowly.

Ligaments

Ligaments are structures that connect one bone to another, imparting stability. Because they are soft-tissue structures that hold hard bones together, they need to be resistant to stress. That's why they are composed of cells called *fibroblasts* that are contained in a matrix of mostly collagen fibers with some elastic fibers, all arranged in a dense parallel pattern. A ligament's ability to heal, if injured, is largely dependent on its blood supply. Some ligaments, such as the medial collateral ligament (MCL) of the knee, are able to heal with proper conservative treatment (in other words, they can often heal without the need for surgery). Other ligaments, such as the anterior cruciate ligament (ACL) of the knee, have no ability to heal and may require surgical reconstruction if torn. The most commonly injured ligaments are the talofibular ligament of the ankle, which is torn during a common ankle sprain, and the anterior cruciate ligament of the knee, which is commonly torn during sports such as skiing and basketball.

Tendons

A *tendon* is a structure that attaches a muscle to a bone. It is similar in structure to a ligament and is built to withstand tensile (pulling) stresses. Despite the fact that tendons have to stretch, they are composed of only about 10 percent elastin—the body's flexible tissue—so they can stretch by up to 10 percent of their resting length. After that, the cells begin to rupture, or tear apart—less easily if the tendon is conditioned, more readily if it's unaccustomed to stress. Age is an important factor in the resiliency of tendons. After age 30, the strength and stretchability of tendons diminishes by as much as 20 percent, a deficit that can be corrected with proper conditioning.

The most common type of stress your tendons experience is known as *traction*, or *tensile stress*. If you hold a rubber band in your fingers and pull it from both ends, you're subjecting it to traction. Keep pulling and you can begin to see tiny tears (microtears) forming along the fibers. The best example of what can happen if those tears accumulate without having a chance to heal, grow, and recover is Achilles tendinitis, a daunting injury that can be disabling to a runner. With enough rest, the tears can heal and the tendons will remain strong. But add an extra mile to your routine instead of gradually building up, or change the surface you run on from something like a dirt path to concrete or pavement (which sharply increases the impact to your foot and heel), and those little tears get bigger. They don't heal in time for your next workout, so the site of the torn tissue expands until eventually you're limping when you get out of bed in the morning.

Joint Capsules

A *joint capsule* is a tissue structure that surrounds a joint, the area where two bones come in contact with one another. It consists of fibroblasts in a matrix of irregularly arranged collagen fibers and elastin fibers. The joint capsule is able to withstand tension exerted in many directions.

The joint capsule should have a certain amount of normal stretchiness. If it is too tight, motion of the joint will be restricted. If the joint capsule is too stretched out, the bones of the joint will be able to slip out of place, resulting in a *subluxation* (partial dislocation) or *dislocation*.

Joints

Joints, or *articulations*, are places in the body where bones come together, allowing you to move when you have to or be still when you have to. Joints are classified into several different categories, but most of the joints that come to mind in the limbs, such as the shoulder and knee, are *synovial joints*. Synovial joints are characterized by a fluid-containing joint cavity that separates the bones. Typically, synovial joints contain articular cartilage, a joint capsule, and a *synovial membrane* that produces something known as *synovial fluid*, the body's natural lubricant. Joints can also contain other components, including ligaments, articular *discs* (menisci), and *bursae*.

Joints have an architectural simplicity to them. Some, like the *interphalangeal joints* that form your fingers, are hinges that move primarily along just one plane. Others, like the hip, are *ball-and-socket joints*—they can move through three planes. In general, however, the greater the freedom of motion a specific joint design permits, the less inherent stability it provides.

The knee, for example, functions as a fulcrum that transfers energy to and from the lower leg for kicking and locomotion, but it also provides a sturdy base of support for standing still. As a result, its design balances stability with range of motion by employing a design known as a *condyloid*, or hinge. The end of the femur (thigh bone) is shaped like a cam with a notch at the center. The ligaments from the end of the femur crisscross within the notch and also attach along either side, tying the bone securely to the tibia (lower leg bone). This design gives the knee a range of about 150 degrees of forward and backward motion (known as *flexion* when you bend it, and *extension* when you straighten it) and 15 degrees of side-to-side rotation— enough to allow you to sit on the ground cross-legged or cut across a field, but not so much that you'd wobble when trying to stand still.

Just as joints are perfectly suited for certain functions, they're terribly unsuited for others. The shoulder, with its great range of motion—some 16,000 degrees in total—must sacrifice stability for mobility in its design.

It's not meant to handle heavy or repeatedly stressful loads. If your shoulder is subjected repeatedly to large arcs of motion under stress (as occurs when one pitches baseballs or swims aggressively), it can overwhelm the stabilizing soft tissue. This is why the shoulder can be so problematic for pitchers, tennis players, and swimmers. The knee, on the other hand, does quite well with compressive forces; it can handle up to 2,000 pounds of up-and-down pressure. But *torque*—the twisting force where the lower leg turns one way and the upper leg another—can tear the knee ligaments apart, as many an unlucky skier can relate.

Muscles

The muscles that move your body are made up of cells called *muscle fibers* due to their elongated shape. Muscle cells themselves are composed of smaller structures called *myofilaments*, which contain important proteins, including *actin, myosin,* and *titan*. The bonds that form and break between these proteins cause the contractions that move your body.

While joints are the fulcrums in your body and bones are the levers, muscles and tendons are the cables. They operate like telescoping drawbridges, with thousands of fibers lengthening or shortening in response to nerve impulses sent by the brain. Each muscle has a specified number of *motor units* (a collection of fibers stimulated by one nerve). For example, the calf muscle has nearly 600 motor units waiting to receive messages from the brain; each unit in turn controls nearly 1,800 fibers. *Precision units,* such as the muscles of the eye, have nerves that control only three to five fibers each, allowing for much more refined movement.

Muscles are encased in tight membranelike structures known as *fascia* and are divided into different types of fibers that are recruited for different intensities of activity. There are many kinds of fibers, but the primary categories are *slow-twitch* and *fast-twitch*. Slow-twitch (or *oxidative*) fibers are adapted for low-intensity endurance activities such as distance running, cycling, and walking. These fibers are slow to act and slow to fatigue but have a high capacity for generating abundant amounts of ATP, as they function by using aerobic metabolism. Fast-twitch (or *glycolytic*) fibers, which are more explosive, are recruited for short bursts of high-intensity activities, such as jumping, sprinting, and weightlifting. These fibers fatigue more quickly but allow for powerful muscular contractions. Fast-twitch muscle fibers use predominantly anaerobic metabolism for energy production.

Different muscles have varying percentages of the two muscle fiber types. Some muscles in our body are specifically designed for endurance, such as the muscles in your back that are responsible for holding your trunk in an upright posture. These muscles contain predominantly slow-twitch muscle fibers. Other muscles, such as the biceps brachii muscle of the upper arm, are built for quick, explosive activities. These muscles contain an abundance of fast-twitch muscle fibers.

Muscles are categorized by the functions they perform. *Flexors* are muscles that decrease the angle between two adjoining limbs. Contract your biceps, and the angle at the elbow joint between the forearm and the humerus (upper arm) decreases. The hamstrings are flexors of the knee; they close the angle between the lower leg and the thigh.

Extensors are muscles that increase the angle between two bones. The triceps muscle extends your elbow joint, and the quadriceps extend your knee. Some muscles, such as the hamstrings and the gastrocnemius (calf muscle), are *biarticular*, meaning they perform different functions at two different joints. Biarticular muscles are generally more prone to injury, particularly when the movement involves the muscle stretching at one end while simultaneously contracting on the other.

In addition to flexion and extension, muscles can perform other functions, such as pronation and supination, the rotational motions that allow your forearms to turn your hands palms-up or palms-down and allow your ankles and feet to roll in and out. *Adductor* muscles move limbs in toward the centerline of your body, as when you bring your arm in toward your side. *Abductors* move limbs away from your centerline, as when you raise your leg out to the side at the hip. Muscles are also capable of causing rotation about a joint, such as can occur at the shoulder or hip.

Other Structures

Several other forms of tissue also play an important role in movement.

Bursae

Bursae are liquid-filled sacs located in or near the joints of the body. They ensure that soft tissues—usually tendons—glide easily in enclosed spaces

KJ Fact: Muscle and Tendon Injuries

- *Strains:* Tearing of the fibers of the muscle–tendon complex, usually at the muscle–tendon interface or the tendon–bone junction. Strains are graded according to the percentage of fibers torn. Partial tears of the muscle–tendon complex are usually associated with significant inflammation—thus the origin of the term *tendinitis*, which means inflammation of a tendon. If there is a complete tear of the muscle–tendon complex, it is referred to as a rupture.

- *Contusions:* An injury to the muscle fibers that occurs when another individual or an object bangs against the belly of the muscle. Contusions rupture the muscle fibers and blood vessels, which leak fluid into the surrounding area, causing a pooling of blood known as a *hematoma*.

- *Myositis ossificans:* A bone deposit that forms within muscle tissue. The condition is caused by a deep contusion that can injure the lining of bone underneath the muscle (*periosteum*), causing calcium to seep into the muscle, where it forms a bone chip.

- *Compartment syndrome:* Muscles are wrapped in fascia, dense sheets of connective tissue. These form compartments that are sensitive to increases in pressure. Compartment syndrome occurs as a result of excessive swelling in the closed compartment. Acute injury causing bleeding or overuse causing swelling increases the pressure within the compartment, leading to pain, numbness, and in rare emergency cases, even paralysis.

where they pass over bones. However, when a nearby tendon becomes inflamed as a result of injury or overuse, or when the bursa itself is subjected to stress or a blow, the sac swells with liquid and, rather than easing motion, it begins to obstruct it. This leads to a cycle in which the inflammation becomes more pronounced, and the spaces in the joint become tighter and more painful. The most commonly affected bursae are the *olecranon*, on the edge of your elbow; the *infrapatellar*, near your knee; the *subacromial*, by your shoulder; and the *trochanteric*, a bursa located near your hip joint. *Bursitis* is also common in the foot, where it manifests as bunions, and near the Achilles tendon behind your ankle.

Proprioceptors

Proprioceptors are tiny sense organs located in your muscles and joints that function as messengers, delivering information between your brain and muscles. The information is related to *kinesthetic* awareness, which means, literally, "movement awareness." These organs enhance your coordination and agility. Three important types of proprioceptors are the *muscle spindles*, which give the brain information about the length of the muscle and the rate at which that length is changed; the *Golgi tendon organs* located at the junction between the muscle and the tendon, which signal muscles to relax, or give up when the degree of resistance is too great; and *joint receptors*, which inform the brain about a joint's position and the amount of stress it is bearing.

After an injury, proprioception is diminished, and decreased proprioception in turn often means an increased likelihood of injury. This is one of the reasons why ankle sprains, even those in which the soft tissue is completely healed, can recur. The proprioceptors are part of the warning mechanism for impending injury.

KJ RECOMMENDS: Bandage Solution
Elastic bandages can help improve proprioception after a knee or ankle injury by cueing your brain to heed sensory signals from the area.

Proprioception can, to some degree, be learned and unlearned. We know this because athletes who had been highly coordinated lose their kinesthetic awareness after an injury and then relearn it by performing special proprioceptive drills.

Fatigue causes a decline in proprioceptive ability, and that decline can lead to an increased incidence of injury as well. There is, of course, an important lesson here: Don't play or exercise through fatigue, because your chances of incurring injury are greatly increased. Aging seems to also cause a natural decrease in proprioception, a possible explanation of why falls are so common among the elderly. Routine exercise may prevent age-related decreases in proprioception.

4

Principles of Athletic Fitness

While participating in a sport is an important part of fitness, no single activity will properly balance your muscles or condition your heart and lungs in a way that adds up to total fitness. In fact, single-minded devotion to a particular sport can cause muscular imbalances that lead to injury, fatigue, and breakdown.

As you age, therefore, it becomes more essential to adopt a general conditioning program—one that enables you to continue pursuing the activities you enjoy. The components of a general conditioning program include:

- *Cardiovascular exercise:* For maximizing aerobic and anaerobic efficiency. We've already established that there is a natural decline in cardiac function as you age, but it can be offset through targeted exercise.
- *Strength conditioning:* To keep the muscles and tendons strong. Again, it's been proved that the natural decline in muscular strength that occurs with age can be counteracted with regular strength training. In the next section of the book, we'll offer exercises that will help you prevent and rehabilitate from common injuries.
- *Flexibility:* Loss of resiliency in the tendons and within joints is one of the main reasons for increased injury rates. But stretching isn't the same as warming up. We'll explain how a few minutes of stretching goes a long way toward preventing injury.

Your fitness program should be designed to help you achieve your individual goals. A fitness program geared toward becoming physically fit, such as for weight loss or improved heart function, will be structured differently than an exercise program aimed specifically at helping you meet an athletic goal, such as improving your tennis game or your running pace.

Principles of Exercise

The general adaptation syndrome discussed earlier in this book offers some basic principles you can apply to any form of exercise. These include:

- *Overload:* In order to reap benefits, whether to your cardiovascular system or to your muscles and bones, you occasionally have to increase the amount of exercise stress placed on your body. Do this by increasing, in small amounts, either the *frequency, intensity*, or *duration* of your workouts.

- *Specificity:* Your body's nerves, muscles, and bones adapt in highly specific ways to the physical stresses placed upon them. While runners, cyclists, and swimmers are all cardiovascularly fit, they've adapted to be efficient at the sports they each pursue. It wouldn't be surprising for even an elite runner to get winded swimming, or for a cyclist to become fatigued while running. Specificity is an unforgiving principle: if you're accustomed to running on an indoor treadmill, for example, your body will still have to make adaptations if you decide to take up outdoor running. A good rule to follow is "train the way you play."

- *Reversibility:* Aerobic capacity, flexibility, and muscular strength all begin diminishing as soon as activity levels fall off. In one study, athletes who had 10 years of training lost aerobic capacity after just 12 days of inactivity. In addition, it can take twice as long to regain previous fitness levels once they've declined. Avoid long periods of inactivity.

- *Diminishing Returns:* The sharpest gains you will make in any exercise program occur during the first few weeks of training. After that, the gains begin to taper off as you reach a plateau. This is natural. In one study, males who were placed on an exercise program saw gains of up to 40 percent in their aerobic capacity within just 10 weeks; at the same time, however, the greatest gains occurred in the first few weeks and tapered off as the program continued. When you hit a plateau, vary

KJ TIP: Anything Works

While it may not always be possible to adhere to a regular schedule of fitness and exercise, even mild activity in the form of 30 nonconsecutive minutes of routine activity interspersed throughout the day, can result in health benefits and can significantly reduce your risk for heart disease. Take the stairs, not the elevator; park a few blocks from your destination; walk when you can; do manual housework.

your program. Either make moderate changes in frequency, intensity, or duration, or change to a new activity.

The Energy for Performance

To supply you with your energy needs, your body uses one of the three metabolic systems outlined earlier: the ATP-PC system, the lactic acid system, or the aerobic system. These systems differ in their proximity to the muscles and the amount of fuel that is available for use. Imagine a company that supplies products to a large city. To meet the immediate needs of their customers, the company will keep a small quantity of products in a small but expensive warehouse in the city. They'll have a larger storage facility uptown that they can get to fairly quickly. But the bulk of their inventory, where massive amounts of products are kept, is in a cheap but rambling location on the outskirts of the city.

When you exercise, the compound that provides the energy for your muscles to contract is adenosine triphosphate (ATP). Run out of ATP, and you run out of steam. If you suddenly need to execute an explosive movement, like leaping for a rebound, reaching for a sharp return in tennis, or kicking the ball across the field in soccer, your body reaches into the "local warehouse"—right inside the muscles themselves—and uses a chemical known as phosphocreatine, or PC, to manufacture ATP. However, the muscles contain less than 30 seconds' worth of ATP-PC, which is why you can't keep repeating explosive movements without fatiguing rapidly.

The second energy system—your uptown warehouse—produces ATP via the lactic acid system. Here you've got an additional three minutes or so of intense power. When you take a hill on your morning run and start gasping for air because your muscles aren't getting enough oxygen, the lactic acid system is what keeps you going. It produces ATP by drawing on stores of glycogen, which is derived from your intake of foods rich in carbohydrates. This form of energy is often called anaerobic glycolysis, because you're burning glycogen in the absence (*an-*) of oxygen (*-aerobic*).

In addition to being limited in how much ATP it can produce, anaerobic glycolysis also causes burning muscular fatigue as a result of lactic acid buildup. If you're unfamiliar with the feeling, climb several flights of stairs two at a time; that paralyzing sensation you get in your quadriceps is lactic acid buildup. When it happens, you need to rest until circulating blood can clear the acid away.

The third type of energy is provided by the aerobic system. In this case, oxygen is pumped in from that faraway storage facility on the outskirts of town—and while it comes slowly, it also comes in abundant supply. If you're jogging at a low to moderate pace, your body can use oxygen to keep resynthesizing ATP seemingly forever (your main limiting factor will probably be dehydration, not lack of energy). In addition, the major waste product formed by aerobic activity is carbon dioxide, which is easily exhaled. (In fact, when exercising, a good way to increase the efficiency of your breathing is to focus less on inhaling deep breaths and more on exhaling fully.)

Measuring Exercise Intensity

Whatever benefits you're hoping to get out of exercise, you can only earn them if you exercise at the proper intensity. There are two main ways to gauge intensity of exercise. The first is by exercising at a certain percentage of your maximum aerobic capacity ($\dot{V}O_2$max). As your $\dot{V}O_2$max can only

KJ FACT: Three Energy Systems
- *Examples of activities that utilize energy from ATP-PC:* Jumping for a rebound, striking a tennis ball, baseball pitching, Olympic-style lifting, kicking a ball.

- *Examples of activities that utilize energy from anaerobic glycolosis:* Sprinting around a track, running up a hill, running up a flight of stairs, running the length of a court or field.

- *Examples of activities that use aerobic energy:* Running, cycling, and any activity that lasts more than a few minutes.

be determined by undergoing a maximal exercise test in an exercise physiology laboratory, this is not a widely used method. The preferable method is to use a percentage of your predicted maximum heart rate (MHR).

If your main goal is weight loss, you're best off exercising at a low to moderate intensity, which is about 60 to 75 percent MHR. At this level, your body burns a higher percentage of fat calories than it does when you exercise at higher intensities. In addition, you can maintain a low to moderate effort for much longer than an intense effort—and for weight loss, duration counts a lot. If you wanted to increase your endurance at a higher level, or vastly improve your aerobic capacity, you'd have to exercise at a higher level of intensity—between 75 and 90 percent MHR.

To monitor the intensity of your exercise using your heart rate, simply check your pulse on occasion by lightly placing your forefinger on the pulse point under your wrist or on your neck just below the jaw. Count the beats for six seconds, and multiply by 10. (In the next few pages, we will give you formulas to help you interpret the intensity of your effort based on your heart rate.)

Alternately, you can purchase a wireless heart rate monitor for about $100. Put on the lightweight chest strap and wristwatch display, and you'll get constant feedback of your heart rate. One of the surprising things you might find is that you overtrain more than you realize; in fact, most athletes find themselves using a heart rate monitor not because it helps them train hard but because it keeps them from training too hard. Another useful function of a heart rate monitor: it can help you chart your recovery time after exercise or between intervals, which can be an important component of an exercise program. How quickly your heart returns to its resting level indicates its resiliency and fitness.

The first figure you'll need to know is your maximum heart rate, which is a function of age, not fitness. We're all born with a high maximum heart rate, estimated to be about 220 beats per minute, and that figure declines by about one beat each year. So, to figure out your age-predicted MHR, subtract your age from 220. (Because this number is just an estimate and can be off by as much as plus or minus 20 beats a minute, you may at some point choose to find out your true maximal heart rate. Your physician or a qualified fitness trainer can help by having you undergo a 10-minute treadmill test.)

The *Karvonen method* is a more accurate measure of how hard you are (or should be) exercising, because it takes into account not only your maximum heart rate but also your resting heart rate, which can be changed by increases in fitness levels and certain medications. When you use this calculation to measure intensity, the guidelines are slightly different than if you use your age-predicted maximum heart rate.

To use the Karvonen method:

- Calculate your resting heart rate. Resting heart rate is your pulse when you're completely relaxed and is generally a good measure of fitness. The average resting heart rate is between 60 and 90 beats per minute. The best time to measure it is first thing in the morning, before getting out of bed. Measure it five days in a row, then average the numbers to get an accurate measurement.
- Subtract your resting heart rate from your true or age-predicted maximum heart rate. This measurement is known as heart rate reserve (HR reserve).
- Calculate the intensity (percent MHR) you want to work at—somewhere between 55 and 85 percent, depending on your goals.
- Add that number to your resting heart rate.

Using a 35-year-old man with a resting pulse of 60 as an example, the numbers would work out as follows:

- Resting heart rate = 60
- Maximum heart rate (age-predicted) = 185
- $185 - 60 = 125$ (heart rate reserve)
- $(55\% \times 125) + 60 = 129$
- $(85\% \times 125) + 60 = 166$

This individual's target heart rate will be between 129 and 166 beats per minute (bpm).

Regardless of which system you use to measure your level of exercise intensity, you can target your workouts in the following ways.

Low to Moderate Intensity

For low- to moderate-intensity aerobic exercise (which is the preferred range for weight loss and general fitness), aim for 60 to 75 percent MHR (50 to 70 percent HR reserve). These workouts range from 30 minutes to two hours or more. A rambling weekend hike, jog, or bike ride can turn such a workout into LSD (long, slow, distance) workout.

Shorter low-intensity workouts—those lasting between 30 and 60 minutes, can be used for active recovery. These sessions are extremely important, because they allow your body to cement the gains made during more intense workouts and keep the body primed without stressing it. Do an active recovery workout the day after a particularly hard session, or when you're feeling dragged out, stale, or otherwise undermotivated.

Don't underestimate the value of low-intensity exercise. It improves your body's ability to burn fat and clear away lactic acid and causes physiological adaptations in your tendons, muscles, and ligaments that allow them to grow in endurance. Studies have shown that if you're among those people who enjoy low-intensity workouts and know how to moderate your activity so that not every workout is an aggressive one, you'll be much more likely to stick with an exercise program.

Moderate to High Intensity

This intense level of "steady-state" exercise (so called because your body, while working hard, is steadily using primarily aerobic fuel) is ideal for building and maintaining a base of cardiovascular fitness and endurance, and for improving your aerobic capacity. Some of the best athletes in the world, including championship German rowers and Kenyan runners, perform the vast majority of their training sessions at this level of intensity. Steady-state exercise is essential for long-term improvements in the functioning of your cardiovascular system. It thickens the capillaries (allowing for more blood and oxygen to pass through them) and improves the function of mitochondria (the energy storehouses where ATP is produced). Do steady-state exercises for a period lasting between 20 and 60 minutes, at 75 to 90 percent MHR (70 to 85 percent HR reserve).

High Intensity

High-intensity training (greater than 90 percent MHR and 85 percent HR reserve) serves several purposes and can take any of several forms. The purposes include:

1. *Speed:* If you're accustomed to running an eight-minute-per-mile pace on your morning 30-minute jogs, it may be difficult to consistently increase your speed. More likely, you'll settle into your accustomed pace for months or years. High-intensity training, usually done using interval training (which we'll explain in a moment), provides you with a methodical way to increase your speed.

2. *Aerobic capacity:* Once you exhaust the fuel from your aerobic supply, you're working on anaerobic fuel, which will deplete fairly rapidly. There is, therefore, a threshold between your body's use of aerobic fuel and anaerobic fuel, which exists at about 85 to 90 percent of your maximum heart rate. If you can raise that threshold, then you can get your body to perform more intensely while still using oxygen for fuel. Clearly, that's a desirable goal.

3. *Sport-specific improvements:* If you're involved in a sport such as tennis, basketball, or soccer, then you're concerned with the sort of endurance that can get you through repeated bouts of high-powered sprints and charges without too much fatigue. Moderate aerobic activity alone won't do that; you need some sprint or interval training.

Raising Your Anaerobic Threshold

Anaerobic threshold (AT) training is designed for the specific purpose of eliciting training effects that increase your ability to perform athletically at a high level. It's not about weight loss and it's not about general fitness; it's simply about increasing your body's capacity for using oxygen to fuel the muscles.

First, recall what the anaerobic threshold is: the level of intensity at which your body's fuel system switches over from one that is primarily aerobic, or oxygen-based, to one that also uses glycogen (is primarily anaerobic). For example, let's say that at your current level of fitness, when you exercise at anything higher than 85 percent of your maximum heart rate, your body begins to go anaerobic. That's when you begin gasping hard for breath, the lactic acid begins to build up, and you're two or three minutes away from stalling out. If you occasionally train at that level, you've begun to condition your body to utilize oxygen more efficiently than before, and your anaerobic threshold will rise slightly but significantly. AT training can improve your aerobic capacity by up to 8 percent.

Forms of High-Intensity Exercise

Once you're actually above the anaerobic threshold and using anaerobic fuel, of course, you can only exercise for about two or three minutes before becoming completely exhausted. However, if you exercise anaerobically for a short duration, rest for a couple of minutes, and then resume your workout for another short burst, you can make some important gains in your athletic performance and fitness. This type of workout takes various forms, including repeats, tags, intervals, or fartleks. What they all have in common is that for a brief period of time, you bring up the pace to all-out levels of intensity; recover; and then repeat. *Tags* is the term favored by cyclists, particularly mountain bikers, who occasionally need to "power up" in order to traverse short stretches of hills or other difficult terrain.

Fartleks, a Swedish term meaning *speed play*, is used by runners to describe similar random snatches of high-intensity work thrown into an otherwise low or moderate steady-state workout. Fartleks don't have to be timed. If you run in an urban area, you can gauge fartleks by lampposts, storefronts, or even the distances between trash cans. Run at high intensity for a brief sprint; then come down to a jog. Do this repeatedly.

When the term *interval* is used, it generally refers to something much more structured—specified periods of time or distance that are done repeatedly during a workout. Between the intervals, you rest (known as the recovery period), catching your breath and giving your blood a chance to clear away the lactic acid. Interval training is ideal if you play basketball, soccer, baseball, tennis—nearly any field or court sport that involves repeated brief sprints.

An interval workout begins with 10 to 20 minutes of warm-up. You then measure out the intervals in time or distance. Working out on a running track obviously makes it easier (most of them are a quarter-mile, or 400 meters).

For example, you can pick a distance of 200 meters, or half a lap. Run hard for the first half, then jog or walk the other half to recover, then repeat six to eight times. Or set a stopwatch to a time period between 30 seconds and 5 minutes, then sprint and recover in equal doses, or jack up your recovery time to two or three times your workout time. Unless you're a competitive athlete, you can feel your way to the proper intervals intuitively. It all depends on how fit you are and how long your work intervals are. A good formula is to pick an interval time and intensity that elevates your heart rate to 95 to 100 percent MHR; once you hit that target, stop. Pick a recovery time that allows your heart rate to return to about 50 percent MHR, and then repeat. Pace yourself so that your performance during each interval is fairly similar (though, of course, you'll be more fatigued at the end).

If you're unaccustomed to hard sprints—even if you're otherwise in shape—your first few sessions of interval training will come as a painful shock. The first set won't be that bad; subsequent ones will hurt and will be significantly slower. But that's OK; intervals are meant to be uncomfortable. You're working in a zone that's beyond your body's capacity to provide your muscles with oxygen. As a result, you're actively depleting your glycogen supplies and causing lactic acid to pool up in your muscles. But you'll reap useful rewards:

- Improved maximum aerobic capacity
- Increased muscle mass
- Increased blood volume
- Inproved heart muscle resiliency
- Increased speed
- Variety

KJ FACT: Target Heart Rate

Intensities of exercise based on using age-predicted maximum heart rate to calculate target heart rate (THR):

- Low intensity: 60 to 74 percent MHR

- Moderate intensity: 75 to 84 percent MHR

- High intensity: 85 to 90 percent MHR

- Anaerobic level: 90 to 100 percent MHR

Target Heart Rates Using Heart Rate Reserve (Karvonen) Method

Note: Heart rate reserve takes into account your resting heart rate (see page 48); these calculations used an average RHR of 60 bpm. To properly use this method, measure your own RHR and adjust accordingly.

Age: 25

Estimated MHR: 195

Percentage	Heart rate per minute	Heart rate per 10-second count
100	195	33
95	188	31
90	182	30
85	175	29
80	168	28
75	161	27
70	155	26
65	148	25
60	141	24
55	134	22

Age: 30

Estimated MHR: 190

Percentage	Heart rate per minute	Heart rate per 10-second count
100	190	32
95	184	31
90	177	30
85	171	28
80	164	27
75	158	26
70	151	25
65	145	24
60	138	23
55	132	22

Age: 35

Estimated MHR: 185

Percentage	Heart rate per minute	Heart rate per 10-second count
100	185	31
95	179	30
90	173	29
85	166	28

(continued)

(continued)

Percentage	Heart rate per minute	Heart rate per 10-second count
80	160	27
75	154	26
70	148	25
65	141	24
60	135	23
55	129	21

Age: 40

Estimated MHR: 180

Percentage	Heart rate per minute	Heart rate per 10-second count
100	180	30
95	174	29
90	168	28
85	162	27
80	156	26
75	150	25
70	144	24
65	138	23
60	132	22
55	126	21

Age: 45

Estimated MHR: 175

Percentage	Heart rate per minute	Heart rate per 10-second count
100	175	29
95	169	28
90	164	27
85	158	26
80	152	25
75	146	24
70	141	23
65	135	22
60	129	22
55	123	21

Age: 50
Estimated MHR: 170

Percentage	Heart rate per minute	Heart rate per 10-second count
100	170	28
95	165	27
90	159	27
85	154	26
80	148	25
75	143	24
70	137	23
65	132	22
60	126	21
55	121	20

The Rating of Perceived Exertion (RPE) Scale

As your fitness level increases, you can begin to sense your training intensity without relying much on percentage of maximum heart rate and heart rate reserve. Several interesting studies have shown that among people who are well-acclimated to physical activity, subjective perception—how one feels—can be an accurate measurement of aerobic intensity.

The rating of perceived exertion (RPE) scale is a tool commonly used to gauge the correlation of a person's subjective feeling of effort to an objective physiological standard of exercise intensity. By using the RPE scale, you can begin to apply the programs we provide for increasing endurance, $\dot{V}O_2$max, and other parameters of aerobic fitness. But we recommend you still occasionally check yourself using the maximum heart rate or heart rate reserve method, just to make sure you're not overdoing or underdoing your workouts.

The RPE scale works on a system of ratings numbered 6 through 20 (the numbers were chosen because they are multiples of average heart rates correlated for the various intensities cited—60 to 200 beats per minute). To use the system, identify the level of exertion you feel during exercise.

Rating number	How it feels	How it relates to your age-predicted MHR
6	No exertion at all	Below 50 percent
7–8	Extremely light.	50–60 percent (warm-up and cool-down)
9–10	Very light (warm-up/recovery)	60–70
11	Light (low-end aerobic threshold)	70–80
12–13	Moderate (aerobic zone)	60–80
14–15	Hard (high-end aerobic zone)	80–90
16–17	Very hard (peak lactate or lactate tolerance)	90–100
18–19	Extremely hard (very, very hard—you're working on anaerobic power)	100
20	Maximum all-out effort with absolutely nothing held in reserve	100 percent until exhaustion

5

Complete Athletic Conditioning

Athletic conditioning involves a mind-set in which the focus of your fitness program is performance. Your goal is to move more efficiently and gracefully with a reserve of energy that allows you to avoid fatigue, and a reserve of strength to prevent injury. The foundation of your program should be the strength and fitness of your heart, lungs, and circulatory system (cardiovascular conditioning). But you'll want to supplement these activities with strength and flexibility exercises that you'll be able to do at home or in the gym.

Cardiovascular Conditioning Activities

The activities recommended for improving your cardiovascular system are those that engage the large muscle groups in a rhythmic and continuous fashion. Some of these activities are described in detail in this chapter. Because different gains can be achieved from performing such activities, it helps to clarify your objectives at the outset. Exercising specifically for weight loss can be done effectively at a low to moderate level of intensity with a high frequency and duration—(at lower intensities you can exercise up to six days a week, but if your intensity level is more vigorous, perform fewer weekly workouts in order to avoid fatigue and injury). Exercising for the specific purpose of increasing your aerobic endurance or your ability to perform without fatigue in a particular sport may require that you exercise at higher levels of intensity and for varying durations.

To achieve the fitness benefits of cardiovascular exercise, the recommended frequency is three to five exercise sessions per week. If your program includes two or less sessions per week, you probably will not make significant gains in aerobic capacity. On the other hand, cardiovascular programs performed too frequently or too intensely are associated with an increased risk of musculoskeletal injury. Find the balance that suits you.

KJ FACT: Wear and Tear

In one minute, at an average rate of 45 to 50 beats, the heart of a well-conditioned person pumps the same amount of blood as an inactive person's heart does in 70 to 75 beats. Compared to the well-conditioned heart, the average heart pumps up to 36,000 more times per day, 13 million more times per year—that's a lot more wear and tear.

Running

Running is an accessible sport that can be done anytime, anywhere. The only cost involved is investing in a good pair of shoes. However, running is associated with a high incidence of lower-extremity stress injuries. During running, your muscles must function as shock absorbers to protect your joints as you land. In fact, from a biochemical perspective, the act of running can be thought of as a repeated series of controlled falls.

Dedicated runners are among the most injury-prone of all athletes. If running is your main form of exercise, you have a 37 to 56 percent chance of sustaining an injury each year, and your chances for a recurrence of that injury are as high as 70 percent.

Two factors to consider in avoiding running-related injuries are the surfaces you run on and the shoes you run in. Both can play an important role in how much impact is transmitted to your joints with each stride.

Above the Surface

The type of surface you run on affects your susceptibility to injury. Concrete and asphalt are hard and unyielding and can add to the force that jolts your joints. Cinder, dirt, low-grass, and pine-covered trails or rubberized tracks are much more forgiving, as are indoor treadmills. Tarred roads are good for running in the spring and summer when they're softened in the warm weather, but during cold months the injury rate on these surfaces increases as well.

Another caution: sloped or banked roads. Most public roads are slanted to allow for drainage during rains—and even if the incline is subtle, it can have marked effects on the biomechanics of your form and may lead to chronic knee and ankle injuries. A banked road creates a situation that simulates having one leg longer than the other. If you run on a track, banking at the turns can have a similar effect, so change directions from one workout to the next. Finally, frequent beach running can be problematic for some people. The heel lands below the surface of the sand, which can contribute to Achilles tendinitis.

KJ FACT: The Best Aerobic Exercise of All

Science substantiates the health benefits of walking. As we mentioned earlier, a Kenyan tribe known as the Massai subsist on a diet that is 70 percent saturated fat—the very animal products that Americans refer to as a "heart attack on a plate." Not surprisingly, autopsies of tribespeople show high levels of plaque in their arteries. What is surprising, however, is that even with the cholesterol and the plaque, heart disease itself is virtually absent from the Massai population, even though they are not vigorously active; they merely walk a lot, and as a result their arteries expand to accommodate the flow of blood despite the formation of plaque deposits.

A recent Finnish study showed that among active and inactive twins, those who walked briskly for 30 minutes only six times *a month* had a 44 percent lower incidence of early death, despite the shared genetics.

Mind Your Shoes

Despite manufacturer's claims, there are no perfect running shoes. Some provide good cushioning but poor stability; others provide good stability but poor cushioning. You'll need to assess which quality is more essential for you.

Normal mechanics for running start with landing on your heel, slightly toward the outside of your foot. Your foot then *pronates*, a motion whereby your arch collapses toward the ground, tilting your foot inward. Pronation plays a very important role in absorbing shock as you land. Its function is to unlock the bones of the foot, dampening the forces transmitted to your body by the ground. As your body weight moves forward over your foot, your weight then is transferred back to the outside of your foot in a motion called *supination*. The function of supination is to lock up the bones of the foot into a rigid structure and to prepare you to push off for your next stride.

Some amount of pronation and supination is normal in running. However, if your foot overpronates or underpronates as part of your running stride, you may be more prone to certain types of injuries. A foot that overpronates is too flexible: the muscles of the leg and foot will be constantly fighting to hold up an arch that wants to collapse. This can lead to soft-tissue overuse injuries in the leg and foot, and sets the stage for chronic back, hip, and knee problems. If you overpronate, you probably need a shoe that has a good, firm midsole imparting stability to the shoe. Some manufacturers market these shoes as having "motion control"—the heel counter (the cup of the shoe in which the heel is seated, extending from the base of the heel to just below the Achilles tendon) will be high and rigid.

People with a high arch in their foot (*pes cavus*) often underpronate; the arch on the inner part of the foot doesn't have enough spring. As a result, there's no give in the foot, so the force of impact isn't absorbed efficiently. If the shock of landing is not absorbed by the foot, it has to be absorbed farther up the leg, predisposing one to stress fractures and Achilles tendinitis. If you underpronate, you may benefit from more damping (cushioning) in the shoe.

Don't look for that cushioning in the bed of the shoe; it needs to be integrated into the construction of the sole itself. How that cushioning is provided is not important if the shoe is well made—some manufacturers use air pockets, others use gel, still others use high-tech forms of shock-absorbent

KJ TIP: Throw Those Shoes Away

The midsoles of even the best-made running shoes usually wear out in as little as 500 miles, so if you're a frequent runner, expect to purchase a new pair accordingly.

foam. The important thing is that it's there if you need it. However, you should ask what part of the shoe contains the cushioning material. Most running shoes have their shock-absorption material in the rear of the shoe only. Some extend that material into the middle portion of the shoe. An added bonus for any runner is forefoot cushioning because of the great amounts of shock imparted to that area of the foot. The ball of your foot is actually where the highest forces are transmitted, not the heel as once thought.

Running Injuries

Most running injuries are attributable to overuse associated with the difficulty of absorbing the shock of up to three times your body weight when you land. Common injuries affecting runners include patellofemoral pain syndrome (often called *runner's knee*), iliotibial band syndrome, shin splints, Achilles tendinitis, plantar fascitis, and stress fractures of the bones of the foot and lower leg.

If you sustain an injury from running, depending on the severity of the injury, cut back on your mileage or take some time off. Use cross-training to maintain your cardiovascular fitness. Try to determine the cause of the injury—a banked road, faulty mechanics, or the wrong type or size of shoe may all be factors. Check your shoes for signs of wear, and replace them frequently. When your injury has healed, work back up to your usual mileage gradually. The recommended rate for increase, if you are interested in increasing your exercise load or working back up after an injury, is 10 percent per week—either in distance or time spent running (but not both simultaneously).

Tips for Athletic Running

- Keep your shoulders relaxed and your upper body erect, not falling forward or hunched over.
- Keep your chin slightly up and gaze straight ahead. It's a simple correction that can improve your overall running posture.
- Keep your fingers loose and relaxed. Wrists should be flush with your forearms.
- Swing your forearms at waist height in rhythm with your pace.
- Think of the motion of your joints and limbs as rolling rather than moving up and down.

- Your feet should hit the ground heel-first, softly and fluidly. If you find your foot slamming down, you may be bringing your striding foot too far forward.
- Let your knee bend slightly as your foot strikes the ground.

KJ TIP: Avoiding Injury

If your running program is causing recurrent injuries:

- Reduce your running mileage—make up the difference with cross-training. Add cycling or other forms of activity to your workout routine.

- Make sure your shoes are the right kind for your needs, and that they fit well.

- Inquire about orthotics. These can be helpful with certain types of bio-mechanical problems, particularly overpronation.

- Modify your technique: work with a coach or trainer.

Cycling

Cycling is an ideal aerobic activity because of its versatility and lower rate of injury. Cycling exerts only half of the compressive forces on joints as running, but it is still a powerful way to increase cardiovascular fitness and muscular endurance. It is often used as a rehabilitative exercise, both to maintain the cardiovascular system and to strengthen the quadriceps muscles which stabilize the knee. Cycling offers great fitness rewards: in one study, lifelong cyclists were shown to have virtually the same muscle mass and function in their later 50s as they did in their early 30s. However, there are a reported 600,000 cycling injuries per year (many of them the result of traumas suffered from falls and collisions), so the sport should be approached with some degree of caution.

Gearing Up

Whenever you're using equipment in sports, the gear functionally becomes a part of your body. In that respect, a poorly sized bike can contribute to poor biomechanics, which will make you susceptible to injury just as a properly sized bike can enhance your riding efficiency. Therefore, purchasing from a specialty shop where an expert can match you with the right bike—whether an outdoor or stationary model—is recommended.

There are several factors to consider in riding form. At the top of your pedal stroke (that is, when the top pedal crank is at twelve o'clock), your thigh should be positioned so that it is angled slightly down toward the ground. When the pedals are at three and nine o'clock, your forward knee should be directly over the axle of your pedal. With the down pedal at six o'clock, your knee should be slightly bent, between 15 and 30 degrees.

There are two primary types of outdoor bikes: mountain bikes and road bikes. Mountain bikes feature sturdier frames, thicker tires, upright seating, and better shock absorption. However, the increased surface area of the tires and the upright riding position mean more air drag and friction when riding. If you live near off-road trails, mountain bikes can provide excellent cardiovascular workouts on flat or hilly terrain. However, downhill riding on steep declines requires some familiarity with riding technique, including proper weighting of the body on different grades, proper braking technique on steep declines, and traversing ("hopping") objects such as rocks, ditches, and logs. Also, keep in mind that riding downhill most likely will not keep you in your training zone for target heart rate.

Road bikes have thinner frames and tires and generally require a bent-over (and thus more aerodynamic) riding position that decreases wind drag. The bent-over position requires that you maintain tension in the lower back and abdomen for proper form.

Other gear considerations for outdoor cycling include pedals and shoes. *Clipless pedals* combine a specially cleated shoe with a small catch on the pedal that effectively locks your foot into the bicycle. It provides a more even pedal stroke in which you're able to provide power on the upstroke as well as the downstroke. These pedals take some getting used to—clipping in and out quickly and smoothly requires a sharp twist of the rear foot, a motion that's best practiced on an indoor trainer.

Another consideration is the seat cushion. Some studies have associated frequent cycling with an increased incidence of sexual dysfunction among men, apparently because the hard, pointy seat used on many road bikes presses against the *perianus* (the area between the scrotum and rectum), which is adjacent to the reproductive vessels. The studies aren't conclusive, but they do warrant that you wear well-padded cycling shorts and choose a gel-padded seat that is comfortable for you. (Again, consulting a specialty bike shop is advisable.) If you feel numbness or pain in the perianal area, consult your physician to determine whether cycling is the cause.

Spinning

Popular new indoor group aerobic workouts that closely simulate outdoor competitive cycling are now available in many gyms under such proprietary names as Spinning, Power Pacing, and others. They're all essentially the same: using sturdy, low-tech stationary bikes, an instructor guides the class through workouts that mimic hills, flats, and downhills.

Cycling Injuries

Some injuries that may be associated with the stresses of repetitive movements of cycling include knee, foot, and ankle problems. These generally afflict "hard climbers" who stand when they pedal or "grind" for long periods of time at high gear. If you use clipless pedals, the angle at which you are locked into the cleat may twist your foot in a way that's biomechanically unnatural for you. Again, a bike specialist can help you size correctly. (A specialist should have you sit on a high bench or table with your leg dangling over the edge to make this determination. When clipped into your bike, your foot should be angled to approximately the same degree and direction as is natural for you.)

Numbness in the forefoot, or *paresthesia*, may be caused by shoes that are laced too tightly. If loosening the shoelaces doesn't work, you may need a cycling shoe with a larger, more cushioned toebox (the upper part of the shoe which encloses the forefoot). Most cycling shoes are, for better or worse, fairly tight in this area because it prevents wasteful movement during the pedal stroke.

If you've had patellofemoral problems (pain that may generate from under the kneecap or just to the side of it) and you're experiencing pain while cycling, try repositioning your cleats on the pedal, adjusting the direction of your toes in or out. Also, play with the seat height until you find a position that takes stress off the knee. For some people, a higher seat height requiring less flexion of the knee may alleviate the problem.

If you feel pain or clicking on the outer edge of the knee, the problem may be iliotibial band syndrome. Try pedaling with the foot slightly toe-outward to see if the problem is alleviated.

Cranking, or riding long distances at a high gear, can exacerbate knee problems. A lower gear pedaled at a higher RPM may reduce stress. A good general guideline is to try to do most of your riding at 90 revolutions per minute (RPM). You can calculate your RPM much the same way you do your heart rate. Count the number of revolutions you pedal in a 10-second time frame. Multiply this number by 6 to get your RPM.

Even though the muscles most powerfully engaged during cycling are those of the lower extremity, it's not uncommon for cyclists to experience pain in the arms, hands, shoulders, and back. When riding, the muscles of the back—including the trapezius, erector spinae, and latissimus dorsi—are isometrically contracted in order to stabilize the body position. However, the tension created can lead to pain, numbness, or spasms. Shifting your upper-body position by occasionally varying your handlebar grip can, in many cases, provide enough movement to ease the tension in these muscles. Handlebar drops, extensions, and forearm rest pads provide a variety of options for shifting your position periodically when riding.

Lower-back pain can result from the sustained forward flexed posture of cycling. A conditioning program that strengthens the trunk muscles may help alleviate this problem.

Pain in the hands, wrists, and forearms generally is the result of the jarring impact transferred through the handlebars. Again, shift your grip while riding, and maintain a light rather than tense grip on the handlebar. Gel-padded cycling gloves and sufficient foam padding on the handlebars can help offset related problems.

Among the most serious injuries incurred while cycling are traumatic ones, caused by falls and collisions. The most severe of these is a head injury. It is recommended that you never mount a bicycle, no matter how easy the terrain or short the distance, without appropriate head protection. (Deaths from head injuries have been reported among cyclists who toppled over on their bikes from a standing stop position.) Other trauma-related injuries

KJ FACT: Helmets *Do* Matter
Eighty percent of fatal bicycle injuries are caused by trauma to the head.

include broken collarbones and wrists, both of which can result from breaking a fall with an outstretched hand.

Tips for Athletic Cycling

- Make sure your bike fits your individual size and needs. Among the values to consider are seat height, handlebar height, distance between seat and handlebar, position of the knee in relation to the ankle, and the toe angle of your cleats (if using clipless pedals).
- Maintain good riding posture and a relaxed grip.
- Wear appropriate cycling clothing, including shorts or pants that are padded to protect the perianal area.
- Always wear a helmet.

KJ RECOMMENDS: Helmet Safety Check

Before purchasing a cycling or inline skating helmet, check the box and the inside of the helmet to see that it bears a certifying tag or sticker from one of the following quality-control organizations:

The American Society for Testing and Materials (ASTM)

The American National Standards Institute (ANSI)

The Snell Memorial Foundation (SNELL)

Rowing

Rowing is an excellent exercise for aerobic conditioning with high muscle-group involvement. However, while it's low impact, the repetitive motion exerts stress on the lower back, forearms, and elbows that can lead to injury. Proper form is essential.

Rowing's reputation as a challenging aerobic activity is well-deserved: at the competitive level, you can burn 250 calories in the course of a 2,000-meter sprint, an event that normally takes well under seven minutes. In return, the activity delivers benefits that include muscular development of the legs, back, and arms, as well as excellent cardiovascular improvements. Rowers tend to have a higher bone density in the bones of the spine that lasts well into the senior years if they remain active.

But rowing also involves a considerable amount of technique, even when using an indoor rowing ergometer (colloquially referred to as an *erg*).

Doing the exercise improperly can lead to pain and injury in the knees, lower back, hamstrings, elbows, and wrists.

The basic premise of proper rowing technique is that most of the power should emanate from the legs and buttocks. The back and upper body should provide only about one-quarter of the power during the stroke motion and should in fact be fairly loose and relaxed during most of the stroke. Each stroke is divided into the following phases:

1. *The catch:* Legs are bent into a crouched position, and the upper body is flexed about 15 degrees forward at the waist with the arms extended.
2. *The drive:* The motion begins with a sharp pushoff from the stretchers (pads onto which the feet are placed). The arms remain extended, and the back remains straight until the legs straighten.
3. *The finish:* With the legs extended, the back extends slightly backward (about 15 degrees), and the arms are brought in toward the torso, midway between the abdomen and the pectorals.

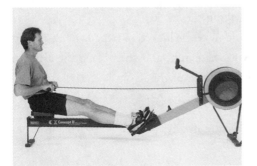

Whether on a machine or on water, the basic rowing motions involve the catch (or push-off), the drive, and the finish (photos courtesy of Concept II Corp.).

Rowing on Water

Rowing is a lifetime sport in which it's not uncommon to find men and women well into their 80s still competing at the recreational level. Proximity to water is, of course, an essential factor, as is access to a rowing club that will make available to its members various types and sizes of boats (or *shells*, as they are commonly called), as well as exercise equipment geared toward improving one's strength and conditioning for the sport. *Sculls* are boats with two oars for each rower; *sweeps* have only one oar for each rower, so athletes generally tend to specialize in either rowing on the port side or the starboard side. The most commonly used shells are eight-, four-, and two-man sweeps, and single sculls.

KJ FACT: Lifetime Endurance

Overall, dedicated male rowers experience little decline in their performance as they age; in his 60s, a male rower can perform at 83 percent of his youthful capacity.

Rowing Injuries

Despite the fact that rowing is technically a low-impact sport, it can produce quite a bit of wear and tear on the body. The most common injuries include:

- Hamstring strain or tendinitis, possibly caused by the imbalance between the quadriceps and the hamstrings. Rowers tend to have highly developed quadriceps.
- Hand blisters, caused by a too-tight grip around the oar handle.
- *Tenosynovitis*, or inflammation of the wrist tendons, also caused by a tight grip.
- Lower-back injury, which may be caused by poor technique in which the back is engaged too heavily in the stroke.
- Elbow injury. The arms should never be locked or hyperextended; keep a slight bend in the elbow at the catch, and then bring the arms in toward the chest only at the very end of the stroke.

Tips for Athletic Rowing

- Keep your head erect and breathe freely; there is a tendency to hold one's breath at the catch.

- Maintain a strong midsection through conditioning to prevent lower-back pain.
- Prevent hamstring injuries by proper stretching and conditioning of the back of the leg with hamstring curls.
- When coming forward on the slide (the track that your seat rides on), don't use momentum to roll forward; instead, contract your leg muscles and move forward in a controlled manner, slowing your body as it approaches the catch.

KJ FACT: A Complete Workout

Rowing is one of the most full-body of aerobic sports. Among the muscles used: the erector spinae, rectus abdominis, gluteus maximus, hamstrings, quadriceps, gastrocnemius, soleus, pectoralis major, latissimus dorsi, serratus anterior, rhomboids, trapezius, subscapularis, teres major and minor, biceps brachii, brachioradialis, and wrist extensors.

Inline Skating

Inline skating is a good athletic activity that can help you develop coordination and balance. However, in order to get aerobic benefits, the activity needs to be continuous and vigorous.

The decade-old sport of inline skating has been shown in studies to have a high aerobic payoff. At a speed of 14 miles per hour, inline skaters who were tested during their workouts showed heart rates that were elevated to 74 percent of maximum, well into the aerobic training zone. At the more vigorous pace of 17.4 miles per hour, skaters' heart rates were elevated to 85 percent MHR, which for many people is close to or above the anaerobic threshold. Calories burned are also comparable to running—between 570 and 1150 per hour, depending upon the intensity of the workout.

Skate Sizing

A comfortably snug skate is essential for productive workouts. The boot, the blade (as the assembly of inline wheels is called), and your foot need to function as one unit for a smooth pushoff and glide. When standing straight, your big toe should be in contact with the front of the boot. With your knee bent and your body in a semisquat position, your foot will move backward in the boot, giving the toe some more room. In addition, on all but the least expensive models, special foam designed to mold to your foot size is used for the inner boot. Before buying, spend plenty of time trying the skates on in a specialty shop to make sure the sizing is right.

There are three primary types of inline skates:

1. *Hockey skates* are sturdy and bulky but provide solid support for quick turns, stops, and short sprints.
2. *Four-wheel recreational skates* are good for covering long distances at a moderate intensity. They are generally full-cut boots made of lightweight materials.
3. *Five-wheel speed skates* are generally cut in an ankle-height boot (though they're available in full-cut boot as well), which may provide less support but offers the potential for greater speed.

Other important factors to consider are the type of buckling or lacing system used (you want to match your individual preference with whichever system gives you a snug fit) and an ABEC rating on the wheels. ABEC (Annular Bearing Engineering Code) is a rating system for quality ball bearings. Wheel size is a factor in how fast the skate is; opt for a minimum of 76 millimeters. Wheels come in two textures: hard wheels are faster, less forgiving, and have less shock absorption but are good for smooth blacktop surfaces. For grainier asphalt, soft wheels are recommended.

Technique

Proper technique is a great barrier against injury—58 percent of inline skating injuries result from poor technique. Inline skating classes are popular and are offered by trainers affiliated with the top skate manufacturers.

Two things to learn: how to fall and how to stop. The instinct on skates, when you feel you're losing your balance, is to windmill the arms in an attempt to regain balance. Inevitably, that results in falling backward, which puts the tailbone (*coccyx*) at risk. Landing on an outstretched arm can result in a fracture or dislocation of the wrist, elbow, or shoulder. Instead of falling backward, instructors recommend that if you feel off-balance, extend your arms out in front of you and lean your upper body slightly forward. Also, bend the knees to lower your center of gravity. At best, you'll regain your balance; at worst, you'll fall onto the parts of your body protected by padding. It should be noted, however, that even with padding and proper technique, there is always a risk of injury when skating.

Stopping on skates requires that you move the braking foot forward and lift the toe, causing the brake pad to come in contact with the ground. Many skates now have brakes that engage simply by moving the foot forward. In either case, the stop is gradual, not sudden, so the possibility of a collision is not automatically precluded. Learning to maneuver comfortably on skates can help you avoid obstacles, cyclists, and other skaters.

Inline Skating Injuries

The most common skating injuries aren't from overuse, but from collision and impact—either with the ground, another skater, a pedestrian, a cyclist, or an automobile. In 1993, there were 31,000 cases of reported inline skating injuries; by 1996, that number had tripled to more than 100,000 cases. (The number of participants, it should be noted, had increased as well—from 12 million in 1993 to 22 million in 1996.)

KJ FACT: It's Always Helmets

Of the 35 inline-skating-related fatalities reported between 1990 and 1996, all were suffered by individuals who were not wearing helmets.

In many cases, injuries can be avoided with the use of safety gear and proper technique. The most essential piece of gear is a helmet. While head injuries aren't the most common skate injuries, they are the ones most likely to lead to death or permanent disability. Avoid using bicycle helmets, which have a large lip of rough foam along the outer edge—the foam may catch on asphalt and twist the head backward, causing a hyperextension of the cervical spine. Ideally, the entire outer surface, up to and including the lip, should be made of a smooth plastic shell. Wrist guards are important as well—the most common of all inline injuries, at 25 percent, are wrist dislocations and fractures. Knee and elbow injuries are less common, but potentially damaging (elbows, in particular, are notoriously hard to heal because of the network of nerves that run through the joint).

KJ TIP: Road Rash Ahead

Road rash, a common inline skating injury, is the painful skin abrasion that occurs when your body slides on pavement. The areas usually affected are the thighs and buttocks. To reduce the odds of getting road rash, wear two layers of shorts when you skate. That way, if you hit the ground, the fabrics will slide against each other, rather than against your skin.

Tips for Athletic Inline Skating

- As you skate, push your stroking leg away from your body—imagine that you're pushing the ground away from under you.
- When you bring the stroking leg forward and back down to the ground, place it as close to the centerline of your body—and the gliding foot—as your sense of balance will allow; the closer in, the more powerful your pushoff.
- Bring your skate down in a controlled manner; push off quickly once the wheels touch the ground.

KJ FACT: Skating Woes

Percentage of total inline skating injuries by location:

- Finger: 5.5
- Wrist: 24.2
- Hand: 3.6
- Elbow: 7.6
- Arm (lower): 13.5
- Arm (upper): 0.7
- Shoulder: 4.2
- Leg (lower): 3.8
- Leg (upper): 1.1
- Knee: 6.8
- Ankle: 6.7
- Foot: 1.0
- Toe: 0.2
- Pubic region: 0.8
- Torso (lower): 5.1
- Torso (upper): 1.8
- Neck: 0.8
- Head: 4.1
- Face: 7.1
- Mouth: 1.2
- Eyeball: 0.2

Source: National Electronic Injury Surveillance System of the Consumer Product Safety Commission

- Relax the upper body.
- You can pump with the arms, but don't involve the shoulders too much—it wastes energy.
- Focus on pushing off by engaging the hip and thigh muscles rather than the calf and foot muscles.
- Learn proper stopping techniques and practice them at slow speeds under the supervision of a friend or trainer.

Swimming

Swimming is a full-body activity that particularly emphasizes the upper extremities, providing good muscle tone as well as cardiovascular benefits. Though it offers a risk of shoulder impingement syndrome, swimming generates the lowest impact of any aerobic sports.

Of 11 major sports surveyed, swimming was found to be the least likely to cause injury of any sort. There are exceptions: shoulder impingement, sometimes called *swimmer's shoulder*, can result from repeated overhand motions. Swimmer's shoulder can be minimized with proper stretching and strengthening exercises targeting the back and shoulder muscles (these are described in detail in Chapter 13, "The Athletic Shoulder"). Also, the whip kick used in the breaststroke can lead to knee injury.

Different Strokes

Making swimming an athletic and challenging workout involves diversity in form and understanding the basic movements and equipment used for in-water training. If you are inexperienced, expect to spend weeks or months on perfecting technique before being able to accrue any aerobic benefits. You may want to join a Masters swimming program to get some instruction from a qualified coach. Even many experienced swimmers are burdened by poor habits that must be unlearned and replaced by proper form. A swimmer with good technique can achieve twice the distance per stroke as a novice, regardless of their respective levels of conditioning.

To integrate swimming into an exercise program, it's advisable to master these four basic strokes: freestyle (also known as the crawl), backstroke, breaststroke, and butterfly.

Water Gear

Workouts can also be enhanced with such training paraphernalia as a kick-board (for drills that focus on kick technique), pull buoy (to help you iso-late armstroke technique), and swim fins (for building strength of the lower leg muscles). Caution should be taken not to use hand paddles, as they can actually contribute to shoulder injury.

KJ FACT: Skip That Nap

Afternoons may be the best time for swimming. Research shows that a swimmer's performance is nearly 4 percent better at 5:30 P.M. than at 6:30 A.M. Overall, late afternoons are better than mornings.

Swimming Injuries

The breaststroke may cause or exacerbate knee conditions, because the sharp whip kick causes an outward twisting of the lower leg bone, creating stress in the knee joint. The same movement can also cause pain higher up in the inner thigh along a muscle known as the adductor longus, which also can be strained by this motion.

Among the most common swimming injuries is swimmer's shoulder, or shoulder impingement syndrome, which is described in detail on page 162. The pain feels as if it emanates from the front, the top, or deep within the shoulder, and is usually associated (depending upon the individual) with a specific arc in the stroke. This pain is a sign that something is wrong, and it should not be ignored. Your stroke mechanics may be causing a problem, or it may be a result of simple overuse.

KJ TIP: Cool-Down

After a vigorous swim workout, cool down for a few laps at a very light intensity— it's more effective at clearing fatigue-related lactate from your muscles than is stopping your workout suddenly.

Tips for Athletic Swimming

- Your hands should enter the water at an angle, not flat. They should slice the surface cleanly.

- Maintain a steady, rhythmic kicking pace; keep a slight bend at the knee, and drop your feet no more than 18 inches below the surface of the water.
- Your head position will affect the position of your entire body in the water. The water level should be just above your forehead, or at hairline level. Keep it too high, and your body will sink below the surface.
- Instead of trying to breathe by lifting your head high out of the water, time your breathing so that you inhale as your body rolls to the side. This creates a small air pocket on the surface of the water—known as a *bow wave*—that enables you to inhale comfortably without upsetting the horizontal movement of your body.
- Your arm pull should create an S-shaped curve under your trunk.
- Keep to a minimum hip movement, choppy leg kicks, or uneven arm pulls, all of which create additional water friction.

KJ CLOSEUP: Get the Rope

Jumping rope can provide you with a portable cardiovascular workout, exercising the upper body in concert with the lower body. It is also effective at expending calories while enhancing speed and coordination.

- To choose a proper-length jump rope: step on the center of the rope and raise the handles to your chest; they should reach a height midway between your chest and shoulders.
- Many people find it more comfortable to jump wearing shoes that do not have a prominent heel counter, such as running shoes. Flatter-soled aerobic or cross-training shoes may be more comfortable—in particular, shoes that have ample forefoot cushioning.
- Strive for a pace of about 100 skips per minute—you'll burn the equivalent number of calories as running approximately seven miles per hour.
- Keep your pushoffs light and soft to minimize impact and stress to the feet, ankles, and shins.
- Stretch adequately afterward to prevent cramping and soreness, paying particular attention to the calves.

Circuit Resistance Training

For all-around strength and cardiovascular conditioning, circuit resistance training is a time-efficient form of exercise. However, it requires access to an array of exercise equipment. Also, keep in mind that for this type of training to qualify as aerobic exercise, you must reach and remain at your target heart rate intensity. You may want to monitor your heart rate regularly when you first begin this type of training to ensure that you are getting the aerobic benefits that you hope to achieve.

Circuit resistance training involves the use of weight exercise stations (such as Nautilus, Cybex, or free weights) to work all the muscle groups in rapid succession. It's distinguished from standard weight training in that the amount of rest allowed between sets is minimal (generally around 15 seconds), the weights are light, and each of the muscle groups is exercised in rapid succession. The primary benefit of circuit resistance training is that it combines a strength workout with a mild aerobic workout in one session, elevating the heart rate while stressing the muscles.

KJ FACT: Pump Up to Weigh Down

Thirty minutes of circuit resistance training burns only about 125 calories, the equivalent of a light jog or brisk walk. However, since it increases your percentage of muscle mass, it improves your overall ability to burn calories even at rest, a benefit that can translate into increased weight loss.

One way to perform a circuit workout: plan on doing 12 exercises, using a weight that allows you do to 10 to 15 repetitions at each station within a time frame of 30 to 60 seconds per set. After finishing at one station, move on to the next one with no more than 15 seconds rest between sets. Perform the entire circuit three times.

Circuit Resistance Training Injuries

Injuries related to circuit training are rare if the exercises are done properly. In fact, circuit training should help you avoid injuries, as you are strengthening all parts of your body. However, one thing to watch out for is impingement of the shoulder. This is a common injury that can occur as a result of any activity involving lifting weights. Be sure to adjust all machines you use to suit your height and the length of your arms and legs.

Tips for Athletic Circuit Resistance Training

- Breathe in when lowering the weight, and breathe out when raising it. Don't hold or "save" your breath for a powerful exhalation—it can momentarily send your blood pressure dangerously high.
- For the upper and middle back, use the lat pulldown machine and the seated row machine. Find the grip and bar that's most comfortable for you. A closer grip will put more stress on the biceps, while a wider grip puts more stress on the latissimus dorsi (in your back).
- For the shoulders, do the military press. Use a grip slightly wider than shoulder width, lower the weight slowly, and raise to full extension.
- For the chest: Try the bench press or fly for the pectoralis major. Closer grips emphasize the triceps; a wider grip emphasizes the large chest muscles. Be careful not to let your elbows drop below the level of your chest. This puts an unnatural stretch on the front of the shoulder joint and can lead the tissues to stretch out over time. Ultimately, this can lead to shoulder subluxation or even dislocation.
- For the hip and groin, do adduction and abduction exercise. Make the movements slow and even. Keep the exercise within a comfortable range of motion. You should feel a mild stretch, if any, at the end of the range of motion.
- For the upper thigh, do leg extensions for the quadriceps (the knee extensors) and leg curls for the hamstrings (knee flexors and hip extensors). Be careful not to lock your knees.
- For the upper thigh and lower leg: Do the leg press or partial squats for the gluteal, quadriceps, hamstrings, and calf muscles. Move the weight

Bench press (photo courtesy of Cybex Corp.)

Back extension

Leg press

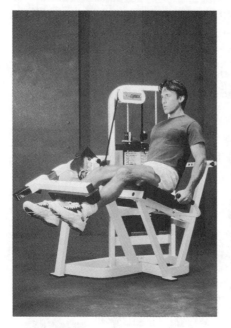

Leg extension

Biceps curl

Resistance exercises using weight machines (photos courtesy of Cybex Corp.)

slowly and evenly; be careful not to lock the knees. Do not bend your knees greater than 90 degrees.

- For the lower leg, toe raises will work both the gastrocnemius and soleus muscles.
- For the arms: Curls for the biceps, extensions for the triceps.
- For the abdominals: Abdominal machine and rotary torso machine for the oblique and abdominal muscles.
- For the lower back: Lower-back machine or extension bench to exercise the erector spinae, which help support the spine.

KJ TIP: How Much Weight Should You Lift?

Because studies about what qualifies as the ideal amount of weight for incurring strength gains remain inconclusive, preferences about resistance training of any kind remain subjective.

One way to find the optimal weight for a circuit training workout is to feel your way there over several sessions. Start with a weight that feels light and easy to handle. Over the course of a week or two, gradually find a range of weight that allows you to lift between 10 and 15 repetitions for each set; by the last repetition, your muscle should be too fatigued to perform even one additional repetition. You may find that the weight you use will eventually be equivalent to 30 to 50 percent of the maximum you can lift with that muscle group for one repetition (a measurement called the one repetition maximum, or 1RM). For example, if your 1RM for the bench press is 100 pounds, then the weight used for circuit training would likely be between 30 and 50 pounds.

Strength Conditioning

The science of strength training is based on the principle of *progressive resistance overload*. If you gradually increase the amount of load you're accustomed to handling, the fibers of your muscles will adapt by becoming thicker and more numerous. This increase in size and strength is called *hypertrophy*, and it is often accompanied by an increase in bone density as well. The phenomenon of hypertrophy has been understood for centuries. An ancient Greek legend tells of a wrestler named Milo who achieved his fabled power by lifting a baby bull over his shoulders each day; as it grew, so did Milo's size and strength.

Muscle hypertrophy occurs as a result of an increase in the number of protein-based units known as *sarcomeres* that make up individual muscle cells. This increase is what leads to the noticeable growth in muscle size you experience when you adhere to a strength training program. Strength training also triggers *neural adaptation*—the ability of your brain to communicate with your muscles. This factor alone (even without the muscle growth) accounts for a sharp increase in strength.

In the 1940s, a scientist named Thomas DeLorme quantified resistance training into a program of sets and repetitions that he used to help rehabilitate injured World War II veterans. His work, which benefited not only those with injuries, but also people weakened with age, has had far-ranging effects on the health, longevity, and performance of athletes as well.

DeLorme's system used lead weights arranged in stacks, which were attached to a cable–pulley system. He had his subjects lift the maximum amount of weight they were able to handle for 10 repetitions. After a brief rest, they performed another set of 10 repetitions, for a total of three to four sets per body part.

Today, DeLorme's concepts remain the basis for the strength training programs used by universities and professional athletic teams. His work also signified a turning point: until DeLorme, muscle development was believed to hinder athletic performance.

How to Train for Strength

A strength training program should include at least eight exercises involving the major muscle groups. The program should be performed two to three times per week with at least 48 hours of rest between workouts. Perform one to three sets of 8 to 15 repetitions of each exercise. Most (70 to 80 percent) of the strength gains you will make from training will come from performing one set of each exercise twice a week. If you are pressed for time and trying to squeeze weight training into your schedule, you can abbreviate your workouts accordingly. When time allows, you can add the additional day and sets for an extra bonus.

Training for strength can be performed using one of three systems: isotonic, isometric, and isokinetic.

Isotonic Training

The most common type of strength training is *isotonic training*. It involves the use of a fixed weight, such as barbells, dumbbells, weight machines, or stretchy bands (see page 89). The weight should be lifted and lowered in a smooth, controlled manner that isolates the muscle being exercised so as to maintain a constant tension on it as consistently as possible.

When you lift a fixed weight, your muscles perform two types of contractions: concentric and eccentric. When the weight is lifted, the muscle shortens to make the angle between the two bones it attaches to smaller. This is a *concentric* contraction. As the weight is lowered, the muscle performs an *eccentric* contraction, contracting as it lengthens to control the weight against the force of gravity.

Eccentric contractions are more efficient than concentric contractions. Thus, your muscles are able to lower more weight than they can lift. If you are training with a fixed weight, you are not sufficiently stressing your muscles eccentrically, as you are lowering the same amount of weight you are able to lift. If you want to stress muscles eccentrically, you need to have some help to lift more weight than you can lift on your own and then lower that amount of weight yourself. As a general rule of thumb, you should be able to lower twice as much weight as you can lift. This type of weight training is often referred to as doing *negatives*. Negatives for the upper extremities can be done by having a partner help you lift a weight, and then you lower it on your own. For your lower extremities, you can lift the weight with both your legs and then use just one leg to lower the weight.

Isometric Training

Isometric training is a form of exercise in which the muscles are contracted without movement of the related joint areas, and thus without a change in the length of the muscle during the exercise. For example, if you pull up on the bumper of an automobile, you won't lift the car, but your muscles will be stressed. You can exercise isometrically by contracting a muscle against itself—for example, by clenching your fist tightly, you can strengthen the muscles of your forearm. Or you can push against an immovable resistance, such as a door jamb. To exercise isometrically:

- Hold the position at maximal contraction (that is, push or pull as hard as you can) for five seconds. Remember to breathe!

- Repeat each exercise for 10 repetitions.
- Do the exercises three to five times a week.

Isometric exercises are frequently used to help rehabilitate an injury, because they strengthen the muscle without requiring movement of the immobilized joint. There is an important caution related to isometric exercise, however: it often involves a momentary restriction of breathing (holding your breath) known as a *Valsalva maneuver*, which refers to air being trapped in a body cavity. (Divers experience it in the eardrums.) It can cause a spike in blood pressure that may dangerous to some individuals.

Isokinetic Training

Isokinetic exercise machines, which (because of their expense) are primarily limited to use in rehabilitation and in professional sports, allow individual muscles to be maximally resisted throughout a range of motion and at specific speeds that are programmed into the machine at the outset. As long as you meet the selected speed of the machine, the machine pushes against you as hard as you push against it.

This type of training has several advantages. First, a muscle's strength varies throughout its range of motion based on its mechanical advantage at different points. However, if you lift a fixed weight, you can only lift the amount of weight that your muscle can handle in its weakest range. With isokinetic training, the speed is fixed. As you get into areas of a muscle's range where the natural mechanical advantage of your joint is better, you can push harder against the machine and the machine gives you more resistance to keep the effort uniform.

Second, there is a safety advantage in isokinetic training. If you were lifting a weight and suddenly experienced pain, your only option would be to drop the weight. If you are training on an isokinetic machine and you experience pain, you stop pushing against the machine—and it stops pushing against you. This is one reason these machines are often used in rehabilitating an injury.

KJ CLOSEUP: Why Strength Training?
- You lose six to seven pounds of muscle per decade after your early 20s; strength training can help you preserve and even increase your muscle mass.

- Strength training promotes neural adaptation; it opens the communication pathways between your brain and muscles so that muscle fibers are recruited more efficiently.

- Strength training increases the energy capacity of muscles by increasing the number of mitochondria, the factories that produce ATP (the muscular fuel).

- Strength training increases your percentage of lean muscle mass, thereby helping your body burn more calories.

- Strength training prevents injury by increasing the resiliency of the muscles and tendons that are used during a particular sport and by strengthening the antagonist and synergistic muscle groups so that no muscle imbalances occur.

Warming Up

Begin each strength training session with light exercise that involves full range of motion and increases the circulation to your muscles. A 10-minute cardiovascular warm-up will increase the temperature of your tissues, making them more pliable and thus less prone to injury. You may want to follow that general warm-up with some sport-specific warm-up that mimics the actions you will be performing in your workout, at a lower intensity than what you will do in your workout.

Flexibility Conditioning

Flexibility refers to the ability to carry a joint through its full range of motion, and it is needed to help you move fluidly and effectively. All muscle–tendon units have a perfect length at which they can be most efficient. If the unit is too tight or too flexible, it has to work harder to get the job done.

As with other fitness factors, there is a genetic component to flexibility; some people are perennially tight and find it challenging to touch their toes, while others have no trouble contorting themselves into seemingly impossible positions. In addition, within each individual, certain joints are highly flexible while others may be tight. Even one particular joint might have flexibility in one direction, but not in another, creating an imbalance. This is sometimes seen in the shoulders of professional baseball pitchers or tennis players. In order for these athletes to be good at what they do, they need to have an excessive amount of rotation in their pitching or racket shoulder. To get the extreme amount of rotation necessary, the front part of the shoulder becomes stretched out. At the same time, the back part of the shoulder tightens up, resulting in a flexibility imbalance. In most situations, flexibility is a desired trait, although too much flexibility may indicate weakness, instability, and susceptibility to injury in a particular joint.

Stretching, which will improve flexibility, should follow a warm-up and should precede both your cardiovascular training (apart from the light warm-up) and your strength training. Unlike other forms of training, stretching can be done as often as you like. You cannot overdo the frequency, and your body does not need recovery time between bouts of stretching.

Flexibility and Injury Prevention

After age 30, flexibility is markedly decreased—and this is a leading cause of sports injuries among those above that age range. A number of factors combine to cause a significant decrease in flexibility:

- Synovial fluid, which lubricates joints, diminishes.
- The amount of water in all tissues of the body decreases.
- Articular cartilage, which provides a soft, cushioned surface where bones meet at the joints, becomes stiffer and less able to absorb shock.
- The tensile strength of ligaments, which stabilize joints, decreases.
- There is a decrease in the resiliency of tendons, which are the part of a muscle most likely to be injured.

An individual's degree of flexibility also varies with the time of day, and even with the season. You may find that you are less flexible in the morning—indeed, morning exercisers have a higher rate of injury.

Flexibility exercises provide a ballast against chronic tightness and are an important means of avoiding injury. In addition, increased flexibility directly improves athletic performance in several ways:

- It allows for a greater range of motion, which in many cases translates into a capacity for potential increases in power.
- It protects the tissues against injury.

- It reduces postexercise soreness (known as delayed-onset muscle soreness, or DOMS).
- It can speed and enhance the healing process after an injury.

General Guidelines for Stretching

- Always warm up before you stretch.
- Enter a stretch gradually.
- Stretch until you feel a gentle, mild pull. Do not bounce.
- Do not stretch to a point that is painful.
- Hold the stretch for a minimum of 10 to 30 seconds.
- Breathe throughout the stretch.

Types of Stretching

The most common form of stretching, static stretching, requires that you enter a stretch gradually and hold the position for 10 to 30 seconds. (Forcing a stretch can cause tears along the muscle fibers, leading to stubborn, long-lasting injuries.) Each stretch is performed for two to four repetitions. A total of 6 to 10 different stretching exercises are performed during each session. The exercises can be done as frequently as you like, but at minimum should be performed before your cardiovascular and strength training programs. The objective is to hold the stretch at a point at which you feel a gentle tugging or pulling in the related muscle area. Bouncing is not advisable. In subsequent repetitions, you can attempt to gently increase the degree of stretch. However, far more important than the degree of stretch you can attain is proper form. Note that it can take several weeks to attain gains in flexibility.

Passive stretching requires the assistance of a coach or trainer and may lead to an even greater range of motion. The trainer places the body in the proper stretch position using his own force or weight. Sometimes passive stretching is accompanied by contract–relax stretching, in which the person isometrically contracts the related muscle area, then relaxes while the trainer or therapist holds him in the stretch position.

Ballistic stretching refers to a "bounce" type of stretching. It triggers a muscle contraction and may be injurious, although it is used by some athletic trainers.

Single Knee to Chest Lie on your back with knees bent. Grasp your right leg behind the knee and gently pull toward your chest. Hold. A mild stretch should be felt in your lower back. Repeat with opposite leg.

Trunk Twist Sit with legs extended in front of you. Bend right knee and place foot against outer side of left knee. Twist toward your right side, using your left elbow to push against the outside of your right thigh. Hold. A mild stretch should be felt throughout your back and hip. Repeat in opposite direction.

Hamstring Stretch Sit with your right leg extended out in front of you and your left knee bent so that the sole of your left foot rests against your right inner thigh. Gently bend forward from your hips over your right leg, keeping the back of your right knee flat on the ground. Hold. A mild stretch should be felt in the back of your thigh. Repeat with opposite leg.

Quad and Hip Flexor Stretch Stand and hold on to something to keep your balance. Bend your right knee and grasp your right ankle. Gently pull your foot toward your buttocks. At the same time, pull the entire leg behind you, taking care not to tip your trunk forward. Hold. A mild stretch should be felt in the front of your hip and thigh. Repeat with opposite leg.

Groin Stretch Sit with the soles of your feet placed together and drop your knees toward the floor. Place forearms on inside of knees and push knees to ground while gently leaning forward from your hips. Hold. Repeat.

Straight Knee Calf Stretch Stand a few feet away from a wall or other stationary object with your left foot in front of your right. Lean into the wall, bending your left knee and keeping your right knee straight. Keep your back straight and your heel down. Hold. A mild stretch should be felt in the middle of your calf. Repeat with opposite leg.

Bent Knee Calf Stretch Stand about one foot away from a wall or other stationary object with your left foot in front of your right. Using the wall for support, bend both knees, keeping most of your weight on your right heel. Hold. A mild stretch should be felt in the lower part of your calf. Repeat with opposite leg.

Posterior Shoulder Stretch Lift your left arm to shoulder height and bring it across your body just below your chin. With your right hand grab your arm at the elbow and gently pull across your chest. Hold. A mild stretch should be felt in the back of your shoulder. Repeat with opposite arm.

Inferior Shoulder Stretch Lift your right arm above your head, elbow bent back behind you. Use your left hand to gently pull the elbow slightly behind your head. Hold. A mild stretch should be felt in your lower shoulder area. Repeat with opposite arm.

When to Stretch

Ideally, you should stretch all your major muscle groups before cardiovascular and strength workouts. However, since no recovery time is needed between bouts of stretching, you can safely stretch as often as you like (see chart). In addition, it is advisable to stretch for several minutes before and after exercise or sports activity. Never stretch "cold." Stretching first thing in the morning, when your muscles are tight from a nighttime of immobility, can cause injury. Instead, warm up with some light cardiovascular exercise for 5 to 10 minutes. Then move your joints and limbs through their full ranges of motion, and follow that with stretching exercises.

Home Exercise Equipment

Home exercise products are more popular than ever, enjoying an annual increase in sales of about 30 percent. However, the number of people who actually use the equipment they purchase is not very encouraging. According to one study, only one-fifth of all people who purchase a home rower make a habit of using the machine. Treadmill owners fare better: 49 percent still use the machines, as do 42 percent of people who buy stairclimbers.

You don't necessarily need an exercise machine to achieve your fitness goals. You can join a health club, run outdoors, or join a recreational sports team. Indeed, if your primary problem is motivation, owning an exercise machine probably won't help. On the other hand, if convenience is the major factor keeping you from exercising consistently, then a home exercise product might indeed be the solution.

Cardiovascular Exercise Machines

When purchasing a cardiovascular exercise machine, consider the following factors:

- It should involve an activity you enjoy.
- Buy it in person at a store where you can test the machine for comfort, adjustability, sturdiness, and ease of use.
- Investigate the policies regarding warranty, repair, maintenance, and return.
- Consider noise and space factors.

Here are some common types of machines.

- *Treadmills:* According to one study, treadmills burn the most calories for the lowest perceived exertion of any exercise machine. Better models have a welded aluminum frame that is durable and rust- and heat-resistant. The deck should be amply sized and supported by rubber grommets that allow for good shock absorption. The treadmill should be motorized; better, more expensive motors are both larger and quieter. The machine should simulate the natural motion of walking or jogging.
- *Stationary bikes:* The frame should be sturdy, and the seat molded and comfortable. A belt-driven drive train and heavy-duty flywheel both contribute to a smooth, natural feel in the pedal action. Adjusting the tension should be easy and should result in smooth transitions through various intensity levels.

  Stationary bikes are available in both upright and recumbent models. If you have a history of low-back pain, you should consider a recumbent bike, which will better support your back and avoid the back-straining posture of leaning forward over the handlebars.
- *Stairclimbers and elliptical trainers:* Stairclimbers simulate climbing stairs, with one exception—as you step on a stairclimber, the step sinks, so very little force is generated upward through your joints. Newly popular elliptical trainers simulate a cross-country ski motion. In both cases, look for a wide range of allowable motion to isolate various muscle groups (steeper angles hit the quadriceps more prominently, while shallower angles target the hips and lower legs).
- *Rowers:* Look for a comfortable oar handle, smooth chain-driven action, and a wind-resistant flywheel that provides increased resistance the harder you pull. The sliding seat should be molded and comfortable and should move easily up and down the rail. The reach of the oar handle should allow for full extension at the finish, and full compression (without bumping against the front of the machine) at the catch.

Bells and Whistles

The most functional add-on for a home exercise machine is an electronic display that gives you information about the level of exercise intensity, number of calories burned, and the duration of your workout. You also want a variety of workout options available to you, from steady-state to hills and intervals.

A bonus feature in some models registers your heart rate. The display prompts you to enter your age and the target heart rate you want for the session. A comfortable chest strap transmits your heart rate continuously while the machine calibrates your workout on an ongoing basis. As you progress in your fitness plan, you can observe your heart working more efficiently at a lower rate to perform the same intensity of exercise.

Strength Training Equipment

It's difficult to outfit a home exercise room with enough resistance equipment to provide the variety of exercises available at a health club. Neverthless, the primary goals of resistance training—maintaining the strength and resiliency of tendons and ligaments—can be achieved with a product as inexpensive and simple as rubber tubing. You can purchase the tubing under brand names such as Theraband or Sportsband, or you can simply pay a few pennies for surgical tubing sold in a medical supply store. Even an old bicycle tire will do. The principle is the same in all cases: by looping or attaching one section of tubing to an immovable area, such as a table leg or a doorknob, and another section around one of your limbs, you can perform a wide range of full-motion resistance exercises. To get the fullest benefits, move through a full range of motion; at the point of maximum contraction, hold for 2 to 5 seconds; then slowly return to the starting position. You can increase resistance by using two straps of tubing instead of one. The recommended frequency is two to three times a week.

Light Weights

Many exercises can be performed with a pair of light, inexpensive dumbbells that weigh 5 or 10 pounds. As a rule, when using dumbbells, begin with one set of 10 repetitions, and do the exercise two to three times per week. When you can do one set comfortably, increase the number of sets to two, with a one-minute rest in between. When you can do two sets easily, increase the number of sets to three. When you can do three sets easily, increase the weight and reduce the number of sets back down to two.

Once you can do three sets comfortably at the new weight, increase the weight again and repeat the cycle.

Set Up Your Environment

The environment you arrange for your home workout area should encourage your ability to get an efficient and intensive workout. Find a place that is well-lit with ample, fresh ventilation. A television, stereo, or reading stand can help pass the time during long-endurance workouts.

PART 2

The Kerlan-Jobe Injury Guide

The following chapters categorize injuries by areas of the body, including the foot, ankle, lower leg, knee, thigh, back, shoulder, elbow, wrist, and hands. When you see references to stretching or strengthening exercises, refer to Chapter 16 where you'll find the exercises described in detail.

6

Coping with Injury

Why You Get Injured

Every force, whether it's intrinsic (coming from movement inside your body) or extrinsic (coming from contact with another person or object) places a stress against your body. These stresses can include:

- *Traction (tensile stress):* Think of pulling on the ends of a rubber band—the stress that eventually causes it to fray at the center is tensile stress. Athletic movement causes the ends of muscles and bones to be pulled in ways that create a similar stress, which can lead to injury if the tissue is too weak or the stress is too great. The Achilles tendon, which stretches every time you walk, run, and jump, is particularly prone to tensile stress.

- *Compressive force:* When you jump, run, or walk, bones in your body collide with one another, much like a stack of fragile plates. Similarly, when your foot is buckled into a ski boot, skiing downhill places a compressive force against the tibia (shin bone). Compressive forces lead to fracture if the muscles protecting the bones are fatigued, or if the pressure is simply too great for the bone to bear.

- *Twisting force:* Known also as *shear force*, it occurs when you rotate any part of your body in opposition to another part or to the ground. Running across a field and stopping suddenly to pivot and turn twists your body in the opposite direction of where your foot is planted; this shear force can damage the ligaments of the knee.

About half of all sports injuries are the result of repetitive microtrauma, or overuse. The rest are due to a traumatic event. Pain, inflammation, swelling, and other related injury symptoms develop slowly over time.

KJ FACT: Injuries

Incidence of emergency-room-treated injuries among popular sports in the United States during one year:

- Basketball: 693,933
- Cycling: 599,874
- Football: 390,180
- Snow skiing: 330,289
- Inline skating: 192,377
- Skating (all types): 322,311
- Baseball: 219,023
- Soccer: 157,251
- Softball: 155,873

- Volleyball: 86,603
- Hockey (all types) 77,140
- Horseback riding: 66,655
- Trampoline jumping: 66,153
- Weightlifting: 57,001
- Golf: 39,928
- Swimming: 36,272
- Tennis: 25,853

Source: National Electronic Injury Surveillance System of the Consumer Product Safety Commission

---

Signs that an overuse injury may be impending include:

- Mild pain after a workout
- Stiffness in a particular joint or muscle upon first awakening in the morning
- Pain during a workout or while performing a particular movement
- *Point tenderness*—pressing down on an area causes a twinge of localized pain
- Swelling
- Instability
- Snapping, cracking, or crunching feelings or sounds emanating from within a joint

The Process of Injury

Before discussing specific types of injuries, it is important to understand the general processes that relate to injury.

Pain

Pain accompanies most (but not all) injuries. It's transmitted by specialized nerve endings known as *pain receptors*, which trigger an alarm warning in the brain that damage has been incurred.

Inflammation

Most pain is caused by inflammation. Inflammation is the body's natural response to any injury or trauma. It is the buildup of fluid and cells around an injury site, and it is synonymous with swelling. When an injury occurs, fluid from the bloodstream leaks into the spaces between the cells of the damaged tissue (muscle, tendon, cartilage, and so on). Inflammation can be readily visible with obvious causes. For example, an acute ankle sprain will cause rapid pain and swelling. Sometimes the pain and inflammation can have a gradual onset and can be hidden from obvious causes. An example is patellofemoral pain (pain under the kneecap, often referred to as runner's knee).

Whether the injury is acute or gradual in onset, the reasons for inflammation are identical: the brain treats the inflammation like an infection (even though it is not). In doing so, the body attempts to "quarantine" the injured area by sending in small bloodborne cells called *platelets*. The function of platelets is to clot or slow down blood flow. The brain also sends other substances to the injured area. It sends white blood cells to fight infection. It sends histamine, which actually causes the cells in the area to leak their fluid into the spaces between the cells, creating even more excess fluid in the area. All of this excess fluid and cellular matter dramatically block normal blood flow, resulting in pain. In the very early stages of an injury, the inflammatory process helps stop bleeding of the injured tissue, so it's helpful. When inflammation persists, however, the problem is that it can ultimately interfere with movement and healing.

Overuse and Overstress

Even when pain and inflammation seem to come out of nowhere, they are in fact the result of a very predictable cycle of occurrences. For example, when you chop down a tree, the first 99 blows with the axe may not actually fell the tree—the 100th will. But the previous 99 certainly weakened the tree substantially.

Similarly, a runner may run 30 to 40 miles a week for weeks, then one day run one more mile than usual. An extra effort would require additional recovery, but this runner doesn't allow for the extra recovery. So even though the run was not much tougher than usual, the reaction is extreme. He suffers knee pain, which is the equivalent of that 100th blow with the axe.

If your heart or lungs work too hard, you usually know it when you start gasping for breath. But if you work your muscles, joints, and bones too hard, the warning signs are generally more subtle. In fact, quite often musculoskeletal pain may disappear during exercise, even though the damage is being compounded. Or it won't become evident for awhile after exercise. During exercise, the sevenfold increase in blood flow to the muscles and joints temporarily forces inflammation to subside. However, when you stop exercising and the blood flow slows down, the excess fluid slowly collects once again in the injured area, and eventually the pain returns, becoming quite pronounced.

When it comes to overuse injuries, the early signs are so subtle that you have to go out of your way to notice them. For example, morning stiffness and pain can be an indication of weakness or inflammation in a joint. That's because at night, your entire body's blood flow slows down—especially the flow to the muscles and joints. During this time, it is easy for inflammation to build up. So when you wake up, any trouble spots will feel particularly stiff. While most morning stiffness is transient, it's a good time to make note of trouble spots that might be susceptible to injury.

Categories of Injury

Injuries generally fall into one of several categories:

- *Sprain:* Injury of a ligament, the soft-tissue structure or "strap" that attaches two bones together. The injury can range from a mild sprain, where the ligament is partially torn, to a complete disruption (a rupture or complete tear) of the ligament.

- *Strain:* Tearing of the fibers of a muscle–tendon complex. This type of injury can also range from a partial tear to a complete rupture. Muscle strains always occur at the site where stress is most concentrated. Such sites are often the part of the tissue where the muscle tapers and becomes tendon (the *myotendinous junction*) and where the tendon inserts into bone.
- *Dislocation (luxation):* Occurs when the bones that come together to form a joint become separated. This involves stretching of the joint capsule and ligaments.
- *Subluxation:* A partial dislocation of a joint. The bones usually pop back together on their own, but not without causing some soft-tissue damage.
- *Fracture:* A break in a bone.
- *Stress fracture:* Also known as a fatigue fracture, this is a small crack that develops in a bone as a result of repeated stress.

Preventing Injury

Avoid the most common training errors—such as increasing your exercise load too quickly, not warming up properly, or not allowing for sufficient recovery time between hard workouts. Once you've triggered an inflammatory response, you run the risk of falling into a vicious cycle known as *overuse syndrome.* The buildup of swelling and inflammation leads to pain and decreased blood flow. Pain causes the muscles to tighten, which leads to further reduction in blood flow. That leads to more inflammation. It's a cycle that can be difficult to overcome.

The inflammatory response, if it's allowed to continue, interferes with the healing process. In order to heal well, you need fresh blood flow in and out of the injured site. The fresh blood brings in oxygen and nutrients needed to build healthy tissue and carries away waste products and excess fluid that have built up in the area.

Anything that increases blood flow helps decrease inflammation and facilitates the healing process. Heat, ice, ultrasound (a treatment administered by a physical therapist), massage, and even exercise—moderate exercise that doesn't cause pain to the injured area (such as light cycling)—may be of value.

Sport-Specific Warm-Ups: Your Frontline Against Injury

Injuries are most likely to occur either at the beginning of a game or workout, when muscles are cold and tight; or at the end of a game or workout, when they are fatigued and weary. You may therefore reduce your risk of injury by warming up before exercise and sports activities and by retiring before you're completely exhausted. (The majority of ski injuries, incidentally, also occur late in the day.)

As mentioned earlier, warming up is a process of preparing your body for increased activity. It allows the blood vessels to expand; the heart rate to increase slowly; and the synovial fluid to fill the spaces between bones, where they can cushion the impact of activity. In addition, the warm-up raises the temperature of your tissues. This increase in temperature results in an increased pliability in the tissues, which can decrease the risk for injury. A proper warm-up includes:

1. Five to 10 minutes of low-intensity, full-range motions of the major joints and limbs
   - Rotate your shoulders, elbows, and wrists.
   - Move your ankles through a full range of rotations.
   - Very gently and slowly, drop your head backward, forward, then side to side.
   - Rotate your wrists, and manipulate your fingers as if you were kneading a mound of dough.
2. Five to 10 minutes of light cardiovascular activity. (Whatever the activity, focus on moving your body through a full range of motion with a minimum of intensity.)
   - If you're a runner, walk briskly or jog.
   - If you're a rower, push away lightly and slowly with the legs, back, and arms.
   - If you're a cyclist, pedal easily at low gear.
   - For soccer, jog around the field twice.
   - For basketball, tennis, and volleyball, jog around the court four times.

3. Follow the warm-up with 5 to 10 minutes of light stretching involving the muscle groups that will be used.

Treating Injuries

Each injury is as unique as you are. While there are general causes, patterns, and treatments for various conditions, each injury occurs through the prism of your own individual makeup and circumstance. Nevertheless, there are some broad guidelines you can follow for minor pains and injuries.

Cease Activity

If something feels acutely or chronically painful as a result of your activity, then stop doing what you're doing. Pain is most often the result of a tear, rupture, or inflammation, and it signals damage to the tissue of your body. Any pressure or movement is likely to compound the injury, even if it's only a minor one.

R-I-C-E

Your main enemy in the hours following an injury is inflammation. The more swelling occurs, the more affected your tissue will be and the longer it will take to get back to full strength.

To minimize inflammation, immediately begin the RICE regimen. The R is for *rest*, which is self-explanatory. The I is for *ice*. Icing an injury constricts the blood vessels, which serves a dual purpose: it minimizes pain and may reduce inflammation, particularly when used immediately following the injury. Ice should be applied as soon as possible after the injury has occurred, held there for 20 minutes, and reapplied three or four times a day for the first 48 hours.

Don't apply heat during the first 48 hours, and don't massage fresh injuries. Both will increase the flow of fluids that contribute to inflammation.

Follow these guidelines when applying ice:

- Used crushed ice or small ice cubes that can conform to the shape of the injury. A bag of frozen vegetables such as peas or corn also works well, as it can mold well to the injured area.
- Wrap the ice in plastic.
- Place a towel over the skin to prevent the skin from freezing.

- Use an elastic bandage or athletic tape to tie the ice compress over the affected area.

The C in RICE stands for *compression*. Keep the injury wrapped. Athletic tape provides the best, most form-fitting compression; but because it is difficult to apply yourself unless you've had lots of practice, it should be applied by a healthcare professional or athletic trainer (if possible). An elastic bandage is second best in terms of its compressive ability, and Neoprene sleeves are a third option.

The E in RICE stands for *elevation*. Keeping the injured limb elevated above the plane of your heart reduces the flow of inflammation to the injured area.

Heat and Ice

Heat and ice are both extremely helpful in speeding healing, but they are used in very different ways.

Ice increases blood flow by initially slowing blood flow and constricting the blood vessels. Your brain then perceives that area of the body as cold, and sends more blood there to warm it up. The first few days following an injury, ice can be extremely helpful for reducing swelling.

Heat increases blood flow by opening up (dilating) the blood vessels. It can be used beginning 48 to 72 hours after an acute injury. If used earlier, it may increase swelling and inflammation. After two or three days, both heat and ice can be used. Alternating ice with heat (contrast baths) can have the effect of flushing stale inflammatory fluids from the area and bringing in nutrient-rich fluids (see Chapter 17 for more details).

Anti-Inflammatory Medications

Non-steroidal anti-inflammatory drugs (NSAIDs) are sold over-the-counter or via prescription under such brand names as Bayer, Motrin, Indocin, and Aleve. The generic names of the most common NSAIDs are aspirin, ibuprofen, and naproxen sodium. These can also help the healing process by working on two levels. First, as analgesics, they decrease pain. Second, they retard inflammation by temporarily preventing the body from producing platelets. Thus blood can flow more easily through the injured area. It is important to note that for these medications to impart their anti-inflammatory benefits, you need to achieve and maintain a certain level of the drug in your system. Read the labels or follow your doctor's advice carefully.

Movement After Injury

It was once thought that injured joints should be completely immobilized until all swelling and inflammation subsided. That approach is no longer taken in the vast majority of injuries because immobility leads to weakness and atrophy of muscles. Injuries that heal while immobilized are also much more likely to form adhesions and irregular scar patterns that can result in a permanently decreased range of motion. A prominent example is adhesive capsulitis of the shoulder, or frozen shoulder syndrome. This is a condition that can occur in the shoulder of an arm that has been immobilized in a cast or sling. The shoulder does not get moved through its full available motion on a regular basis, and the joint capsule becomes tight due to buildup of scar tissue.

With mild injuries, you can find the proper balance between rest and movement by letting pain be your guide. Increasing circulation with activity will decrease inflammation and help facilitate the healing process. Static isometric exercise, in which a muscle is contracted against itself or against an immovable object while the joint remains immobile, can be used to retain muscle tone and strength if there is no pain. Contract the muscle and hold for a count of 10, then relax. Do 10 repetitions, 10 times a day. As the swelling and inflammation diminish, begin doing light isotonic movements (that is, dynamic resistance exercises) and flexibility exercises. After each exercise session, ice the joint to counter any inflammation.

With more serious injuries such as fractures, immobilization for a prolonged period of time may be necessary. The key to successful healing lies not just in the medical treatment, but also in a comprehensive rehabilitation program done under the guidance of a knowledgeable therapist.

See a Doctor If . . .

In the absence of an obviously serious injury in which bleeding or tissue injury is evident, the question about when to consult a healthcare professional becomes a gray area. The following guidelines may help. See a physician if:

- You suspect a fracture. Emphasis on the word *suspect*: the old rule that if you can move it, it ain't broken, is a fallacy. And because fractures can in rare cases involve a disruption of nerve pathways, possibly resulting in permanent disability, an office visit is imperative.
- You experience a dislocation. Your shoulder pops out, or your kneecap slips off its track. Joints seldom separate without also tearing soft tissue such as ligaments and tendons in the process, even if they pop back in on their own (partial dislocation, or subluxation). Dislocations that aren't properly cared for are liable to recur. And here, too, you have to be concerned that along with ligament damage there may have been injury to a nerve.
- You hear or feel a sudden popping sound. Even with a complete ligament or tendon rupture, pain and swelling, which are the more obvious signs of injury, can be absent for the first 30 to 60 minutes. The feeling that something has snapped, however, accompanied by a sudden inability to bear weight or pressure on the injured area, is a sign of possible rupture. Don't wait for the swelling to start—if it pops, see a doc.
- You experience numbness, extreme weakness in a limb, or tingling that doesn't go away. These are possible indications of nerve damage and demand swift medical attention.
- You experience chronic swelling, weakness, or decreased range of motion around a joint. Chronic injuries deserve a look by a physician if they consistently swell up during or after a workout or are significantly stiffer, weaker, or looser than the opposing limb or joint.
- The pain doesn't diminish with rest. Laying off an injury should lead to a gradual reduction in pain and swelling and an improvement in mobility. If rest doesn't make it better, see your doctor.

7

The Athletic Foot

The foot functions both as a shock absorber when landing and as a lever when pushing off. In both cases, it is the endpoint for large amounts of energy that are the equivalent of as much as ten times your body weight.

A foot that functions poorly influences the movement of much of the body above it. Every bone, joint, and muscle from the base of your foot through the lumbar region of your spine is part of a kinetic chain, a unified linkage in which movement in one area affects movement along the entire chain. For example, your tibia (lower leg bone) rotates clockwise and counterclockwise within the ankle joint depending upon the biomechanics of your foot. Since the bone is also part of your knee joint, its rotation affects that joint as well. And since the femur (thigh bone), which also is part of your knee, rotates in direct opposition to the tibia, it too affects the biomechanics of your foot, as do your pelvis and lumbar spine. As a result, many of the stress injuries and pain syndromes that appear in remote parts of this kinetic chain can be explained, prevented, and treated by making corrections in the biomechanics of the foot.

There are two hinges between the leg and the foot. One hinge is at the ankle, or *talocrural joint*. Motion at this joint moves the foot up into *dorsiflexion* (the toes point toward the shin) and down into *plantarflexion*. The second hinge is located below the ankle and is known as the *subtalar joint*. It provides the all important side-to-side motions of the foot known as pronation and supination. These functions are key in enabling your foot to absorb shock and push off from the ground. Normally, when your foot strikes the ground, you hit on your heel, slightly toward the outer side of your foot. Your foot then pronates, a motion where your arch rolls toward the ground. The function of this motion is to unlock the bones of your foot, facilitating shock absorption. As your body weight moves forward over your foot, your foot rolls outward, or supinates. Supination functions to lock the bones of your foot back up so that you have a rigid platform from which to push off. Some amount of pronation and supination is normal and is required for your foot to function properly. However, overpronation is often associated with flat arches (or "flat feet"), and excessive supination commonly occurs in feet with high arches. Problems with overpronation or oversupination can have wide-ranging effects on the foot, lower leg, knee, hip, and low back, and are usually caused by:

- Arches that are too high or too low
- Muscular imbalance, tightness, or weakness in the lower leg
- Biomechanical problems with the subtalar joint itself

KJ TEST: Pronation and Supination

Try this: Stand on one leg and put your weight over the inner arch of the foot; that's the pronated position. Feel how your foot is springy, poised to absorb shock. However, if you tried pushing onto the ball of your foot while pronating, you'd find you have very little leverage. Now supinate, or shift your weight slightly toward the outer edge of your foot. You can feel how your foot is poised for leverage rather than shock absorption in this position. It's this pronating–supinating motion that allows the foot to serve both as a shock absorber and as a rigid lever.

Structures of the Foot

Here are the important structures that make up the foot:

Talocrural Joint (Ankle)

This is the joint that is created where the two bones of the leg—the tibia on the inside and the fibula on the outside—come together to join with the *talus*, or ankle joint, below. The motions that occur at this joint are dorsiflexion and plantarflexion.

Subtalar Joint

The subtalar joint, located below your ankle, is where the talus comes in contact with your *calcaneus* (heel bone). Its side-to-side motions of pronation and supination allow your foot to absorb shock and function as a lever for pushoff, as well as allowing it to adapt to uneven ground surfaces.

Ligaments

The lateral (outside) ligaments of the ankle include the *talofibular, calcaneofibular*, and *tibiofibular* ligaments. The medial (inner) aspect of the ankle is supported by a strong ligament called the *deltoid ligament*. Both medial and lateral ligaments work together to resist excessive rotational forces at the ankle.

Fat Pads

The fat pad of the heel cushions your initial contact with the ground. It protects the calcaneus (heel bone). The fat pad under the ball of your foot decreases pressure when you push off. The fat pads are made up of thin columns that keep the fat firm and absorb shock even under great impact.

Arch

Also called the *instep*, it is formed by alignment of the heel and metatarsal bones (the long bones of the foot), creating a stable tripod held together by ligaments. Just as the foundation pillars support a building, the arch is the foundation supporting the body's superstructure. Alterations in the alignment of the bones can result in excessively low- or high-arched feet, which are associated with different overuse syndromes of the foot.

Plantar Fascia

The longest ligament in the foot, sometimes called the arch ligament, the *plantar fascia* runs along the bottom of the foot, from heel to toes, and functions as the spring inside the arch. Every time your toes push off the ground, the toes bend upward, tightening the plantar fascia and creating a springboard effect.

KJ FACT:

Even though the heel is the first point of contact with the ground, it's not the one subjected to the most impact. The most impact is transmitted to the forefoot.

Metatarsals

Underneath the thin layer of skin on top of your foot are long, thin bones that run to your toes called *metatarsals*. The thickest and strongest, the one running to your big toe, is the one that functions as the main lever for pushing you off the ground. Changes in bone alignment shifting pressure from the large metatarsal to the smaller ones on the outside of the foot can result in stress fractures. The smallest, thinnest metatarsal on the outside of the foot is also prone to fractures when the ankle is sprained.

Phalanges

The small bones that make up the toes—three each for the four smaller ones, and two bones for the big toe—are called *phalanges*. Their gripping ability and flexibility provide strength and balance during walking and running. They also serve as a site of attachment for the plantar fascia.

Sesamoids

The *sesamoids* are two small bones under the ball of your great toe; they are designed like a miniature version of your kneecap. The downward-flexing muscle of the big toe wraps around the sesamoids, using them as a fulcrum to provide additional power for the big toe.

Posterior Tibialis

This muscle–tendon complex originates in your calf and runs down the inner side of your ankle, just below the *malleolus* (the knob that sticks out

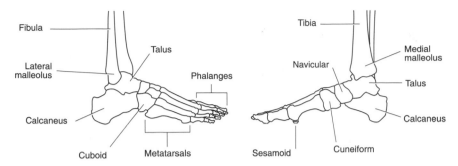

Medial and lateral views of the bones of the foot and ankle

from your ankle). It attaches to several areas in the foot, most prominently the *navicular*, which is a wedge of bone in front of your heel bone. This muscle helps support the highest point of the arch of your foot.

Anterior Tibialis

The *anterior tibialis* is the main muscle that brings the foot upward at the ankle (dorsiflexion). Injury to this muscle's tendon or to the nerve that goes to the muscle can result in foot drop, an inability to control your foot as it lands on the ground.

Peroneal Muscles

Located behind the lateral malleolus (the outside knob of your ankle), the peroneal muscles help keep your ankle from rolling inward.

Flexors Hallucis and Digitorum

A collection of muscles and tendons that curl your toes downward, they originate in the calf, span the foot, and attach in the toes.

Extensors Hallucis and Digitorum

Located opposite the flexors, they curl your toes upward.

Common Foot Problems

Combine repeated stress with a hard surface, poor footwear, and insufficient recovery time, and you may eventually encounter some of the following aches and pains.

Plantar fascitis

Pain at the heel (known as *plantar fascitis*) is caused by inflammation of the plantar fascia, or arch ligament. It's the most common form of foot pain among runners, basketball players, tennis players, and others involved in foot-impact sports. Early signs include pain, stiffness, and tenderness anywhere along the arch or under the heel, particularly in the morning when you take your first steps. Causes include overuse, poor conditioning, ill-fitting shoes, or a tendency toward overpronation. Distance runners tend to have a more gradual onset of symptoms; for basketball players and sprinters, the onset can come suddenly. In chronic cases, painful bone deposits, known as *heel spurs*, form at the site of the attachment of the plantar fascia to the undersurface of the heel bone.

If the earliest signs of the condition—pain, soreness, tightness, or discomfort along the length of the arch—are caught, then adequate rest coupled with gentle stretches may help derail the problem early on. However, once symptoms progress, this condition can take an inexorably long amount of time to heal.

These measures may provide relief:

- Reduce or cease the aggravating activity.
- Apply an ice pack to the arch once or twice a day to reduce pain and inflammation.
- Strengthen the posterior tibialis, which supports the arch and takes pressure off the plantar fascia.
- When sitting at your desk, do toe curls—curl your toes for 10-second counts, 10 times in a row.
- In the morning, before getting out of bed, move your feet and ankles around in circles to increase blood flow to the area. Gently massage the ligament for about a minute by rolling a golf ball along the base of your foot.
- Stretch your plantar fascia and calf muscles.
- You may benefit from more arch support. You should feel close and full contact between the arch of your foot and the support. It should be comfortably worn all day long in daily activities, before you use it for athletics. Supports can be purchased from sporting goods stores as

ready-made devices. Custom supports, or *orthotics*, can be obtained from an orthopedist or other healthcare professional specializing in the treatment of foot and ankle disorders.

Arch Irregularities

- *Pes planus (flat feet):* This condition causes overpronation. The arches themselves may or may not hurt, but related pain and injuries can include iliotibial band friction syndrome, patellofemoral pain syndrome, posterior tibial tendinitis, shin splints, and plantar fascitis. It's advisable to counter the condition by strengthening the muscles that support the arch with toe raises; alternate between pointing the toes slightly inward and outward when doing the exercise. Stretching of the structures of the calf and the plantar fascia may be beneficial. However, the key remedy is to give the arch added support. You may benefit from an over-the-counter arch support as well. If pain persists, see an orthopedist or healthcare professional specializing in treatment of the foot and ankle for custom orthotics.

- *Pes cavus (high arches):* Caused by a chronically tight arch ligament; the tension may force the big toe into a permanently curled position (claw toe). Other common complaints related to high arches include:

  * Tight calves
  * Metarsal pain under the ball of the foot
  * Plantar fascia and heel pain
  * Pain along the top of the foot, which is forced upward against the hood of the shoe as a result of the high, rigid arch
  * Frequent ankle sprains
  * Shin splints
  * Peroneal tendinitis
  * Calluses under the big toe and lesser toes, as well as calluses on top of claw toes

Gentle stretching and soft, shock-absorbing orthotics may help relieve the conditions associated with the rigidity caused by high arches. Rigid orthotics are not indicated in this situation.

KJ TIP: Orthotics

Orthotics are molded inserts that can be placed inside your shoe to provide support or cushioning. Their primary function is to correct the biomechanics of the foot. In some cases, store-bought orthotics are effective. For problems related to flat arches, such as plantar fasciitis, try using a semirigid arch support. For high-arch problems, a softer shock-absorbing orthotic may be beneficial. For heel bruises, a simple cushioned heel cup can effectively relieve the pressure on the calcaneus. In short, flat-arched feet need more support and stability, while high-arched feet require cushioning. Sesamoiditis and pain on the ball of the foot can be relieved with a "dancer's pad," a strip of foam that is placed on the sole of the foot, right behind (not directly over) the ball of the foot.

Experimenting to see which options offer pain relief is no more complicated than placing a folded tissue in your shoe, adjacent to the affected area, and walking around to see if it feels at all more comfortable. If it does, you can then consider purchasing an orthotic. Any orthotic should feel as if it fully contacts and supports your arch. It should be used comfortably for an entire day of casual wear before venturing into using it for any athletic activities. Orthotics are only as effective as the shoe. Replace shoes every six months to give maximum support and cushioning.

Sesamoiditis

Pain at the ball of the foot, or *sesamoiditis*, can be caused by injury to the tissue from excessive mechanical pressure resulting in inflammation. Refrain for one week from running and jumping activities. Relief may be provided by a forefoot pad (called a dancer's pad, available in pharmacies and sporting goods stores) just behind (not directly under) the ball of the foot. A stiff-soled or thick-soled shoe can minimize flexing of the forefoot, which often exacerbates the pain, until the pain subsides. Fractures of the sesamoids are serious and should be diagnosed and treated by a physician; they tend not to heal well without proper care.

Toe Fractures

Toe fractures are usually caused by direct trauma. If one of the smaller toes is involved, it can be splinted by taping it to an adjacent toe until it heals;

if the big toe is involved, it may need to be set and immobilized by bracing or surgical pinning.

Metatarsalgia

Inflammation at the ball end of the metatarsals, or *metatarsalgia*, can be caused by increased mechanical pressure resulting from alteration in bone alignment. It can happen in feet with high or flat arches. For relief, place a metatarsal pad under the area of inflammation in the midfoot to provide support. Run on softer surfaces, and try using a shoe with forefoot cushioning, wide toebox, and low heel counter. A full-length orthotic may help to redistribute the pressure more evenly to other parts of the foot.

Posterior Tibial Tendinitis

Posterior tibial tendinitis is often associated with overpronation. The affected tendon supports the arch and can become tender at a point behind the inner knob of the ankle; the pain is most prominent when the heel is raised. Gentle stretching, ice, and reduced activity or rest can help. Change to firmer, more supportive shoes. Use semirigid arch supports. If pain persists, see an orthopedist or healthcare professional specializing in the treatment of the foot and ankle.

Heel Bone Bruise

The fat pad of the heel and the bone underneath it can become inflamed and sensitive to pressure. Until the pain subsides, minimize weight-bearing on the affected heel. A firm plastic heel cup can compress the fat pad into its original shape and effectively protect the heel bone. Sometimes a cushioning heel pad can be equally effective.

Stress Fracture

Stress fractures are small, microscopic cracks in the bone, usually due to repetitive impact and overuse. The most common bones of the foot involved are the metatarsals. Stress fractures often do not show up on a plain x-ray until the healing process is well under way. A bone scan is sometimes needed for definitive diagnosis. While the injury is healing, avoid all impact activities. Substitute swimming and light cycling for running activities.

Bursitis

The most common sites for inflammation of the foot, or *bursitis*, are at the side of the big toe (where the inflammation is known as a bunion) and at the side of the little toe (known as a bunionette). The cause in both cases is friction from rubbing against the inside of the shoe. Bursal inflammation can also occur at the attachment of the Achilles tendon to the heel bone. For bunions, wear a shoe with a wide toebox; a foam donut can protect the bunion from further rubbing and irritation; and a soft-rubber column, available in pharmacies, can be placed between the big toe and the second toe if they have begun to overlap. In rare cases, where the bunion or bunionette is disabling, surgery can be performed to excise the bony prominence and correct the misalignment of the bones that contributes to the condition.

The bursa near the Achilles tendon becomes inflamed as a result of friction with the heel counter. Changing to a shoe with a different heel-counter height can fix the problem. Persistent heel bursitic pain may require an orthopedic consultation to assess for the presence of calcium deposits and bone spurs.

Morton's Neuroma

Burning pain, tingling, or numbness (known as *transient paresthesia*) between the toes (usually the third and fourth toes) can indicate *Morton's neuroma*. It's common among people who run and use stairclimbers because of exaggerated pressure on the foot, which entraps the nerve. The nerve slowly enlarges due to increased pressure in this area.

To address the problem, loosen the laces of your shoes. Wear shoes with a wide toebox. If you use the stairclimber a lot, shift your foot position frequently. If you wear ski boots or skates often, add padding to the tongue and don't overclamp the buckles. Orthotics may help by redistributing the pressure away from the nerve. Persistent pain may require professional evaluation and possible surgical excision of the enlarged nerve.

Black Toe

Bleeding under the toenail (*black toe*) can be caused by the forefoot jamming against the toebox. Painful black toe due to blood under the nail can be treated by twirling the end of a sterilized paper clip through the surface of the nail to relieve the pressure. There are no nerve endings in the nail itself, so you won't feel any pain. (However, penetrating through the nail and into the deeper tissue is painful.) Black toe can be treated with ice and rest. Shoes should be sized to accommodate the problem of the foot pushing against the toebox. Avoid shoes that are either too loose or too tight, and make sure there is adequate toebox space.

Turf Toe

Pain and stiffness within the big toe, often occurring in conjunction with bone spurs on top of the joint, is called *turf toe*. Pain is aggravated when pushing off, requiring flexing of this joint. Abnormal alignment of this ball-and-socket joint results in excessive wear of the articular cartilage, ultimately causing degenerative arthritis. Choose shoes with more room at the toes and stiff, thick soles to reduce bending at this joint. Professional evaluation is helpful, and surgical treatment may be necessary.

8

The Athletic Ankle

The ankle joint, or talocrural joint, is where the talus meets the bones of the leg (the tibia on the inside and the fibula on the outside). The talus is a trapezoid-shaped bone that is sandwiched between the two bones of the lower leg. The lower ends of the tibia and fibula form the knob-shaped protrusions that most people think of when they picture an ankle. The motions that occur at the ankle joint are dorsiflexion and plantarflexion.

Acting as a hinge joint, the ankle regulates a great deal of movement and force through the foot, but it's plagued by a structural irony. When your foot is poised for its greatest power, fully plantarflexed so that you're up on the ball of your foot (entering a jump, sprint, or other type of pushoff), your ankle is in its least stable position. That's because of the shape of the talus, which is narrower in the back than it is in the front. When you are up on your toes, it is the narrow part of the talus that sits between the tibia and fibula, leaving lots of room for excess motion. This explains why ankle sprains are among the most common of all sports injuries. Particularly common is an *inversion sprain*, in which the ankle turns inward. The relatively small, thin ligaments on the outside of the ankle lend minimal support in relation to the broad, thick deltoid ligament on the inner aspect of the ankle.

Structures of the Ankle

The important structures that form the ankle include the following.

Talus

A trapezoid-shaped bone wedged between the bones of the lower leg. It is covered with ultra-smooth cartilage that allows the bone surfaces to slide over each other, even under great pressure. The upper portion of the talus joins with the tibia and fibula, providing the up-and-down motions of the ankle. The lower part joins with the calcaneus (heel bone) to form the sub-talar joint, imparting side-to-side motion.

Medial (Inner) and Lateral (Outer) Malleoli

These are the bony knobs that are landmarks for the ankle joint. The inner one is formed by the tibia, while the outer one is formed by the low end of the fibula.

Subtalar Joint

This joint, formed by the joining of the talus and calcaneus, operates like the independent suspension of a military vehicle—it finds a way to set your foot down so it's flush with the surface, even if the surface is uneven. The subtalar joint enables your foot to pronate and supinate, the side-to-side motions that assist with shock absorption and provide a stable lever for pushoff.

Syndesmosis

A unique type of joint formed by ligament and fibrous connective tissue that bridges the gap between the lower leg bones just above where they form the ankle joint. If the syndesmosis is loose or damaged, it can dramatically affect the strength and mechanics of the ankle.

Deltoid Ligament

This ligament attaches at three points: the upper attachment is to the medial malleolus, or inner knob of the ankle; it then fans down and out to attach to the talus and calcaneus.

Lateral Ligaments

These ligaments almost always get injured or ruptured when you sprain your ankle and are in fact the most commonly injured ligaments in all of sports. The lateral ligaments connect the fibula to the talus and to the calcaneus. In the typical ankle sprain, the downward and inward position of the foot finds the ankle bones in their least stable alignment. Consequently, the ankle ligaments provide the main support and are vulnerable to injury. Moderate to severe twisting usually injures only the ligaments on the lateral side, but a very severe twisting injury can injure the ligament on both the outside and the inside of the ankle. Ligament injury can occur with or without an associated fracture.

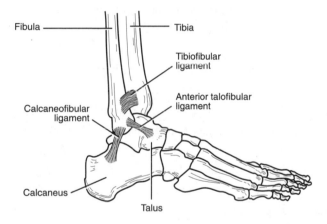

Lateral ligaments of the ankle

Common Ankle Problems

Twists, turns, and sprains eventually take their toll on this vulnerable joint.

Ankle Sprain

Probably the most common sports injury, ankle sprains account for more than 40 percent of all injuries in basketball alone. The majority of cases are inversion sprains—the foot turns inward, stretching and tearing the ligaments on the outer part of the ankle. Severe twisting injuries can affect the ligaments on both the inner and outer aspects of the ankle. Swelling and pain usually originate directly in front of the lateral malleolus (outer knob of the ankle) and become most acute within half an hour after injury. Commonly affected is the talofibular ligament, which holds the smaller bone of the fibula (the lower leg) to the the talus; and, sometimes, the calcaneofibular ligament, which connects the fibula to the calcaneus. A related concern: the impact of an ankle sprain often causes the fifth metatarsal, the long, thin bone on the outer edge of the foot, to fracture. It can also cause a fracture of the lowest part of the outer leg bones (or sometimes even the inner leg bones).

Some of the things that can predispose you to ankle sprains include running or playing on uneven surfaces; wearing away of the outer portion of the heels of your shoes; running in a crossover style, with your striding foot landing inside the centerline of your body; and hiking or running on off-road trails when you're unaccustomed to them.

In the event of an ankle sprain, ice should be applied immediately. Crushed ice is the preferred choice because it's better able to conform to the grooves and indentations around the ankle. The joint should also be compressed immediately. When wrapping the joint, fill out the hollows around the ankle with strips of foam or a foam ankle donut in order to compress the indentations, which are the areas most prone to swelling.

Avoid placing any weight on the ankle for at least two days. After that, and in the absence of any exacerbation of the pain, isometric contraction of the surrounding muscles can be performed. Allow approximately 6 to 12 weeks for healing, depending on the severity of the sprain. All the while,

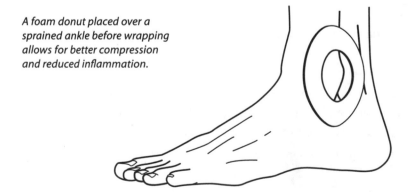

A foam donut placed over a sprained ankle before wrapping allows for better compression and reduced inflammation.

keep the ankle compressed (though not so much that you cut off circulation), and always ice it after doing any kind of exercise.

Once you've recovered, continue supporting the ankle with athletic tape or a brace. These add stability and should allow your ankle its full up-and-down motion while limiting the side-to-side motion, thereby protecting the healing ligaments. Initially, you may have to avoid activities that require quick side-to-side motions of your foot. Stretching, strengthening, and proprioceptive drills are all essential to successful rehabilitation of the joint. An ankle fracture can occur under similar scenarios, but the resulting pain and deformity are both more intense and more obvious. Ice, wrap, and immobilize the joint immediately and seek medical care.

KJ TIP: Should You Wear an Ankle Brace?

Wear an ankle brace or support if you have a history of ankle sprains or ligamentous laxity. The brace may help not only by directly supporting the ankle, but also by increasing the "volume" of ankle proprioceptors, in effect enabling them to be better heard by the brain.

Syndesmotic ("High Ankle") Sprain

A less common form of ankle sprain, this injury causes separation of the syndesmosis, as well as ligament damage. The pain, usually localized over the outer malleolus, can be intense, and swelling or deformity may be evident under the skin. The injury occurs as a result of the tibia violently rotating inward while the foot is planted. In very severe cases, there may also be injury to the deltoid ligament, and possibly fracture of the fibula at midleg. Syndesmosis sprains and fractures require immediate medical attention.

Osteochondritis

If a bone-and-cartilage chip comes loose and floats into the ankle joint, it will get caught in the hinges, causing the joint to click, lock, or become inflamed. The pain feels like it's coming from deep inside the joint. There may be swelling, limited range of motion, and pain when you dorsiflex the foot. In about two-thirds of the cases, the cause is a sprain, twist, or fracture of the ankle. The fragment can be surgically removed through arthroscopy, but sometimes the chip gradually diminishes in size and disappears on its own.

9

The Athletic Lower Leg

The lower leg is musculoskeletally compact, consisting of two long bones and four muscular compartments (anterior, lateral, superficial posterior, and deep posterior), each of which contains several muscles. The main function of these muscles is to control the active and passive movement of energy through your foot and toes via the ankle joint. Second, the muscles in back of your leg (the posterior muscles) play a role in flexing and controlling the knee during various phases of athletic activity. And third, the muscles provide the fine balance of contractions and relaxations that allow you to stand for a length of time.

Structures of the Lower Leg

Here are some of the important structures that form the lower leg.

Tibia

The tibia, or shin bone, runs along the front of your lower leg. Because it's so close to the surface of the skin, the tibia can easily be damaged by a blunt force, and not necessarily a particularly hard one. Shin guards are, therefore, essential gear for sports such as soccer and martial arts where there's a likelihood of contact to the area.

The tibia flares out at each of its ends. At the top (proximal) end, it forms the knee joint and serves as a support column for the massive femur and all of the body weight. Below, at its distal end, it has a cuplike cavity that sits like a lampshade above the talus, forming the ankle joint. This mortiselike structure has a lip on the medial side (the side that your big toe is on) that extends farther downward and forms the medial malleolus. The lower portion of the tibial shaft, just above the mortise, is the thinnest part of the bone, and is therefore the part most susceptible to fractures.

Fibula

Thinner than the tibia, the fibula's main purpose is to help support the complex of muscles in the lower leg. Like the tibia, the fibula also extends to the ankle and contributes 60 percent of the stability of the joint; and it has a lip that extends downward, forming the lateral malleolus of the ankle, which is tied to the side of the talus with ligaments. The lateral malleolus is about one-half an inch lower than the medial malleolus, which is one reason why inversion sprains are more common than outward-turning (eversion) sprains.

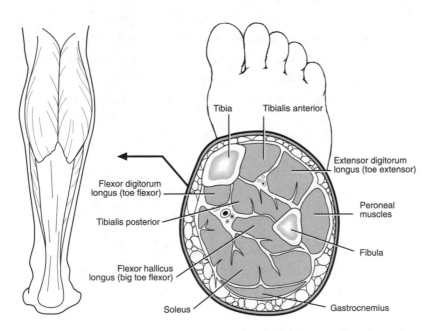

Cross section of the bones and muscles of the right lower leg

Peroneus Longus and Peroneus Brevis

These muscles, which run down the outer part of your leg, raise the outer border of the foot and dorsiflex the ankle. They provide protection against inversion sprains of the ankle by preventing the foot from turning inward.

Gastrocnemius

The calf muscle closest to the surface of this skin, the *gastrocnemius* extends from above the knee to the calcaneus. It assists the hamstrings in flexion of the knee, in addition to plantarflexing the foot.

Soleus

This calf muscle, deeper than the gastrocnemius, assists the gastrocnemius with plantarflexion and is important in stabilizing the tibia during walking and running.

Achilles Tendon

The muscles of the calf—the gastrocnemius and the soleus—drop down toward the heel and connect to the foot via this single, powerful cord of tissue. The gastrocnemius and soleus muscles, working through the Achilles tendon, are the main source of power in plantarflexing the foot for running, pedaling, sprinting, and jumping.

Posterior Tibialis and Anterior Tibialis

The tibialis muscles are located in close proximity to the tibia. *Posterior tibialis* aids in plantarflexion, turns the foot inward, and helps support the arch. *Anterior tibialis* dorsiflexes your foot so that it clears the ground when you swing your leg forward during running or walking. When your foot initially contacts the ground, tibialis anterior is responsible for slowly lowering your foot to the ground in a controlled manner.

Flexors and Extensors

These small muscles control the movements of the toes. *Flexor digitorum* curls the four small toes. *Flexor hallucis* pushes your big toe (the *hallux*), downward. *Extensor digitorum* originates along the tibia, moves down along the top of your foot, and connects to the four small toes, where it pulls them upward. *Extensor hallucis* runs parallel to extensor digitorum and pulls the big toe upward.

Common Lower Leg Problems

Shin splints, calf strains, and other lower leg problems can become chronic and recurrent, so it's important to know when to back off your exercise program and allow adequate time to heal. Here are some of the injuries you may encounter.

Peroneal Tendinitis

If you have high arches or chronically sprain your ankle, the peroneals (longus and brevis) will have to do more work to stabilize the foot, leading to potential inflammation. The pain is felt along the lateral side of your lower leg or ankle. Peroneal tendinitis can also result from an ankle sprain that damages the *retinaculum*, a band of fibrous tissue designed to hold the end of the peroneal tendon in place in a groove behind the lateral malleolus. Among skaters and skiers, the peroneal muscle can also become strained by a forward fall. A chronically weak or inflamed peroneal tendon can make you susceptible to frequent ankle sprains.

Peroneal tendinitis should be treated like any other soft-tissue inflammation. Ice, rest, and compression are the keys to recovery. If the retinaculum is damaged as a result of an ankle sprain, it may need to be repaired surgically. An excellent exercise for targeting the peroneal muscles is wrapping a piece of sport cord or tubing around both of your feet, then turning them outward against the resistance of the cord.

Achilles Tendinitis and Achilles Tendon Rupture

The Achilles tendon is the lowermost channel for much of the impact that occurs when your foot meets the ground. It bears a tremendous load during normal activity, but during sports it's frequently taxed beyond its limits. When that overload continues unabated—particularly past age 30, when tendons start losing their resiliency—the result is small tears in the tendon fibers, which create a syndrome of chronic debilitating pain and weakness. Runners (particularly hill runners and distance runners), and cyclists (particularly "hard riders" who grind long distances in high gear) are among the athletes most susceptible to these types of injuries. Increasing your mileage, wearing different shoes, running on a harder surface than usual, or coming back too aggressively after a long period of inactivity can all predispose you to Achilles tendinitis.

Achilles tendon rupture is a far more debilitating injury. The most likely scenario for a rupture occurs during an activity when you are flat-footed with your ankle dorsiflexed and your knee extended (stretching the calf muscle, which attaches to the Achilles tendon), and you then engage in a sudden, violent eccentric muscle contraction. This scenario places the tendon at its maximum point of stretch at the same time that it's being placed under a heavy load. You will feel, and possibly hear, a big pop in the lower part of the back of your calf. You will probably be unable to put weight on your foot. Basketball and tennis are the most common sports during which this injury occurs.

For an Achilles tendon rupture, immediate medical attention is required. The tendon may need to be surgically repaired. Tendinitis can be treated with rest from the offensive activity for three to six weeks, while adhering to the following program:

- Use ice twice a day.
- Perform light slantboard and wall stretches.
- Perform isometric plantarflexion and dorsiflexion exercises.
- Do toe raises, performing the exercise in an exaggerated slow motion.
- Use a three-eighths-inch heel pad to raise the rear of your foot and take pressure off the tendon (or wear a shoe with a heel about that size). If a heel lift is used, it should be used in both shoes so as not to create a leg length discrepancy, which could lead to other injuries.
- Wear well-cushioned shoes with a low rear heel counter that doesn't rub against the tendon.
- Ultrasound and deep friction massage by a physical therapist may be helpful in favorably influencing the scar tissue that forms during healing to lay down along the same lines as the fibers of the tendon.

Among the preventive measures you can take to avoid this condition:

- If you want to increase the volume or intensity of a workout, do it gradually over a period of weeks.

- Beware when playing or running on a new surface or wearing new running shoes; either can set the stage for Achilles pain.
- Take the pressure off: stick to softer running surfaces like dirt, cinder, or a rubberized track.
- At the first sign of pain, reduce your activities, and apply ice after the workout.

Tibial Stress Fracture

Stress fractures are the result of an accumulation of microscopic cracks along the length of the bone as a result of overuse or overtraining. The lower third of the tibia is a common site of stress fractures in the lower body. The injury doesn't occur suddenly, and neither does the pain. It sets in gradually, over a period of weeks, at first hurting only during or after your workout. (In some cases, fatigue-related fractures in which the body's repair process lags behind the process of bone degradation can be a sign of bone disease, so chronic problems should be seen by a physician.) But if you feel around and press down on the right spot, the pain will feel intense. As a stress fracture progresses, it can graduate into feeling painful at all times. Commonly, stress fractures will be overlooked in standard x-rays. A bone scan may be recommended for proper diagnosis.

Because stress fractures tend to recur, if you suspect you suffer from a chronic condition, you may wish to consult your doctor. You can help prevent stress fractures by following these guidelines:

- Choose soft surfaces such as cinder, dirt, or rubber for running.
- Don't make sudden changes in your mileage.
- Wear shoes that provide adequate shock absorption (and be aware that cushioning in even the best shoes doesn't last through more than 500 miles of wear).
- Condition and stretch your lower leg muscles.

Compartment Syndrome

Compartment syndrome is caused by an increase in pressure within one or more of the four muscle compartments of the leg that are enveloped and separated by fascial (connective tissue) membranes. When you're working out, blood flow within these compartments increases, causing the muscles to expand by as much as 20 percent. If there are further increases in volume of the compartment (as a result of inflammation or bleeding), the fascia may not be able to expand enough. The pressure then increases, leading to pain, tingling, cramping, or numbness. The onset can be sudden (acute) or gradual (chronic). Acute episodes are usually brought on by a direct blow to the shin (contusion) that causes intracompartmental bleeding, or by a sudden increase in the degree of your exertion, which causes injury to the muscle–tendon unit. The most common site for compartment syndrome is the anterior compartment in front of the leg, near the flat portion of the tibia. The condition can cause your muscles to cramp up so tightly that you're forced to stop your activity. Most of the time, as soon as you do stop, the symptoms go away. In extreme cases, the blood flow is so severely restricted that nerve injury occurs, resulting in temporary or even permanent paralysis of the muscle.

For numbness, pressure, or paralysis that aren't immediately relieved by stopping activity, see a physician immediately. The fascia may have to be loosened via an incision to release the pressure. If you suffer from mild, chronic compartment syndrome, in which the pressure, pain, and tingling only occur when you're running or cycling hard, follow these guidelines:

- Reduce your exercise load, and then very gradually build back up.
- Wear better-cushioned shoes and run on softer surfaces.
- If the symptoms continue, you may be helped by a surgical procedure that expands the area of the compartment.

Shin Splints

Shin splints describes a condition of pain and inflammation on the inner and slightly posterior (rear) aspect of the leg (usually along the lower half to third of the tibia) due to overuse of the posterior tibialis muscle. Potential causes include an exaggerated stride (extending your leading leg out too far when you run), distance running on hard surfaces, and most commonly, overpronation. The pain is caused by inflammation at the broad area where the posterior tibialis attaches to the tibia. The periosteum, the thin layer of tissue covering the bone, often becomes inflamed as well. As bone tissue is highly innervated, this condition can be very painful.

Refrain for at least a week from activities that exacerbate the pain. Apply ice twice a day for 20 minutes at a time. When the pain subsides, a semirigid arch support can help limit overpronation, relieving stress on the posterior tibialis. Check your shoes for undue wear that has affected cushioning ability. Run on softer surfaces such as grass, dirt, cinder, or a rubberized track. Choose a shoe with good motion control to help minimize overpronation. Consider custom orthotics to lend support to the arch and modify the biomechanics of the foot.

Gastrocnemius Strain (Tennis Leg)

A *gastrocnemius strain* is a tear of the fibers in the more superficial (closer to the surface) calf muscle. The gastrocnemius crosses two joints, the ankle and the knee. Like other biarticular (two-joint) muscles (such as the hamstrings), it's most prone to injury when it performs two different functions at either end simultaneously—as when you step forward to plant your foot in a position with your knee extended (a move that is common in tennis, hence the name *tennis leg*). The pain is usually sudden and can feel like a sharp ping or pop. (It can even feel as if you've been hit by a pebble.) The area over the injured tissue may immediately turn red and feel hot; you may have trouble raising yourself up on your toes.

If you suffer a strain, immediately begin RICE. It may take as long as two months for a calf strain to heal completely. During that time, switch to conditioning activities that don't place load or impact on the calf muscle. A heel pad or shoe with a higher heel may help take pressure off the calf muscles during recovery. If you play tennis, it is especially important to maintain strength and flexibility in the calf muscles and Achilles tendon. Calf stretching should follow a light cardiovascular warm-up before you hit the court.

10

The Athletic Knee

Along with the muscles of the thigh and lower leg, the knee joint is part of an intricate cable–pulley system that is the basis for athletic locomotion. A well-defined axis of rotation allows the knee to bend and extend a full 150 degrees, a range of motion that you probably won't exploit except under extreme circumstances.

Nevertheless, in sports the knee is the most victimized joint. Biomechanically, muscle imbalances in the thigh can pull the kneecap one way or another; malalignment in the foot or ankle can increase the rotation of the leg bone, putting added strain on the knee. When it comes to injuries sustained from external forces, the knee is particularly unforgiving. Its important fibrocartilage discs—the *menisci*, as well as the cartilage behind the kneecap itself—are not replaceable (though there has been recent progress in the development of synthetic substitutes). The ligaments and cartilage inside the knee are poorly nourished by blood and do not regenerate or heal efficiently on their own.

The knee is really two joints—the *patellofemoral joint* and the *tibiofemoral joint*. The patellofemoral joint is where the patella (knee cap) articulates with the femur (thigh bone). The patella has a ridge along its undersurface. This ridge rides up and down, like a train on a track, in a groove in the femur called the *trochlea* as you straighten and bend your

KJ SPOTLIGHT: Knee Problems

Knee problems occur for one of three reasons:

- *Biomechanics:* The kneecap, or *patella*, rides along a defined track in the femur designed to maximize the power of the quadriceps as they extend the leg. If the patella is misaligned—either as a result of a congenital problem, poor technique, muscle imbalance, or poor mechanics in the foot—it can cause chronic knee pain and inflammation.

- *Impact:* The knee is designed to follow a fairly rigid axis of rotation that allows it to bend and straighten, and not much else. (The side-to-side rotation is minimal.) Any force—whether extrinsic, such as a tackle to the side of the leg, or intrinsic, such as twisting the knee while stepping into a ditch—may result in damage to the ligaments and cartilage.

- *Age and overuse:* Both the back of the kneecap and the ends of the tibia and femur are lined with articular cartilage that can erode or wear away, allowing the exposed bone beneath to eventually become chipped, jagged, and eroded. In addition, age affects the amount of synovial fluid (joint lubricant) produced by the joint capsule of the knee.

knee. The function of the patella is to act as a pulley for the large, powerful quadriceps muscles of the thigh, increasing their mechanical advantage.

The tibiofemoral joint is the larger joint of the knee. The articulation itself is not very stable, so the ligaments and tendons that run over, through, and around the knee do the stabilizing work. Additionally, the menisci impart some stability to the joint as well.

Structures of the Knee

A spare, ingenious design provides the healthy knee with the stability to channel great amounts of force through the lower extremity muscles.

Cruciate Ligaments

Named *cruciate ligaments* because they cross each other in the knee joint, these are the most important stabilizers of the knee. The *anterior cruciate*

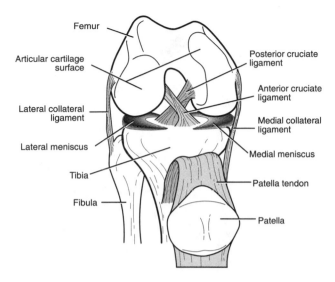

Structures of the knee shown with the knee flexed and patella reflected

ligament (ACL) crosses from the front of the tibia to the back of the femur and prevents the tibia from sliding forward on the femur. The *posterior cruciate ligament* (PCL) runs from the back of the tibia to the front of the femur and keeps the tibia from sliding backward on the femur.

Medial and Lateral Collateral Ligaments (MCL and LCL)

These ligaments add stability to the sides of the tibiofemoral joint.

Menisci

The *menisci* are disclike structures made of fibrocartilage that sit between the femur and tibia. There are two menisci in each knee (medial and lateral), and they serve several important functions:

- They decrease the compressive forces on the knee by spreading out on impact, thereby protecting the underlying articular cartilage.
- They help stabilize the knee.
- They help lubricate the knee joint by spreading synovial fluid.

Quadriceps Tendon

This broad tendon connects the quadriceps muscle to the top of the patella.

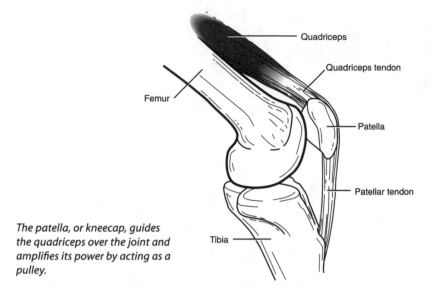

The patella, or kneecap, guides the quadriceps over the joint and amplifies its power by acting as a pulley.

Patellar Tendon

The patellar tendon is a strong strip of tissue that runs from the kneecap to the tibia. You can feel it just below your kneecap—it feels like a strip of lead, is about three inches long, and is the terminal connection between the thigh muscles and the tibia.

Popliteal Fossa

The cavity in the back of your knee that contains many important nerves and blood vessels is called the *popliteal fossa*. It is the juncture of the hamstrings, which control bending of the knee. The top portion of the gastrocnemius also attaches in this area.

Common Knee Problems

The knee is not a joint that recovers well or quickly. Prevention, conditioning, and adequate recovery time are all essential for the joint's proper functioning.

Patellofemoral Pain Syndrome

This injury goes by many aliases. It has been called *kneecap pain, runner's knee, chondromalacia*, and *maltracking patella*. As threatening as it sounds, in most cases it is not a major problem and can be controlled if you understand what it is and what to do about it.

Wherever two bones come together to form a joint, the parts of the bones that contact each other are lined with articular (hyaline) cartilage. This is the type of cartilage that you see on the white, shiny ends of a chicken drumstick. It is different than the fibrocartilage that comprises the meniscus. When you hear the term *torn cartilage* used to describe a knee injury, it refers to the meniscus.

The function of articular cartilage is to absorb shock and protect the underlying bone, which, when damaged even slightly, can be very sensitive and painful. The good news about cartilage is that it can absorb force without hurting. The bad news is that cartilage cannot repair itself because it does not have a good blood supply—so it can slowly wear away, and often does with age and overuse. Major injuries to the cartilage can mean major problems in terms of movement. When it comes to the patella, however, injuries to the cartilage often present only a minor, nagging problem.

One of the important functions of your kneecap is to act as a pulley for your large, powerful quadriceps muscles. As the quads come down from your hip, they narrow to form the quadriceps tendon, which runs over your kneecap before attaching to your tibia. The kneecap, by acting as a pulley, gives your quadriceps better leverage, allowing you to lift, walk, squat, run, and jump better. Overstressing your quadriceps on a regular basis can put excess pressure on the kneecap, causing the cartilage on the patellar undersurface to wear down.

Another factor that may lead to erosion of the knee cartilage is improper tracking of the kneecap. The underside of the kneecap has a central ridge that slides up and down along a groove located on the femur. That ridge happens to be the only area of bone here coated with cartilage. When the patella maltracks—as it does among many people—it becomes like a train that has only one set of its wheels on the track. The set that's dragging begins to wear away.

A partially eroded kneecap will cause pain, because it's unable to dampen the forces exerted on the underlying bone by the powerful quadriceps muscles. Depending on how advanced the condition is, it may hurt only at very specific times, causing a quick twinge; or it may cause inflammation and hurt for longer periods of time.

If your knee is aggravated, it may hurt during squatting, running, or going up or (more commonly) down stairs. Once the patellofemoral joint gets inflamed, it can hurt when sitting or driving with your knee bent, or even at rest following stressful activities. During these times of inactivity, blood flow slows down and inflammation builds, resulting in pain.

Among the possible causes of patellofemoral pain are:

- *Chondromalacia patella:* A condition in which the cartilage behind the kneecap softens.
- *Muscular imbalance:* Two quadriceps muscles that attach to the knee—the vastus lateralis and the vastus medialis oblique—each pull on the kneecap from opposite directions in an effort to keep it properly centered as it moves along the groove of the femur. Most often it's the vastus medialis oblique that's weaker, allowing the kneecap to track too much toward the outside. If the lateral structures on the outside of the knee are too tight, the effect is the same—the kneecap tracks toward the outside. That can cause the equivalent of a partial dislocation (subluxation) and subsequent pain and degeneration of the knee.
- *Poor foot biomechanics:* Overpronation can cause mechanical problems that result in patellofemoral pain.

If the problem is chronic, consult an orthopedist to determine the cause and to provide options that can include knee strengthening and flexibility exercises, or surgical procedures that may help smooth out the cartilage. The best measures are preventive: at the first sign of kneecap pain, refrain from activities that place high compressive forces on the knee—squatting, stairclimbing, heavy-resistance biking, and running, especially downhill. Consider cross-training, substituting exercise that is less stressful to your knee. Good substitutes are low-resistance biking, stairclimbing without deep steps, walking, pool running, and the cross-country ski machine.

Make sure you have proper footwear both for shock absorption and to control overpronation if you have that problem.

Strengthen the muscles that protect your patella. If your muscles can act as better shock absorbers, then less force is transmitted to the irritated cartilage. Treat any inflammation, and use ice after activity.

Sprain or Rupture of the Anterior Cruciate Ligament

A very common knee injury, a tear of the ACL is caused by twisting of the knee with the foot planted, or by trauma, such as a front or side tackle. The injury is extremely common in skiing and may occur when one ski gets caught in the snow while the rest of the body keeps moving. Even though ACL injuries are serious, pain and swelling may not be immediately evident. What will be noticeable is the feeling that something has "popped," and that the joint is inherently unstable. It will feel as if it gives way underneath your body weight.

The injured joint should be iced, compressed, and elevated immediately. If possible, see a doctor soon, as diagnosis is best made before swelling and inflammation have set in. The ligament rupture may require surgical reconstruction, as the ACL is unable to heal on its own due to lack of sufficient blood supply. Surgical reconstruction involves using a tendon from another part of the body, such as the hamstring tendon or patellar tendon, to fashion a substitute ACL. Rehabilitation from an ACL injury can take as long as six months.

Sprain or Rupture of the Posterior Cruciate Ligament

Not as common as ACL tears, PCL injuries generally occur when the tibia is hit from the front while the knee is bent, such as might happen in a car accident where the knee hits the dashboard and the tibia is forced backward. PCL sprains can also occur when the knee is hyperextended.

This injury should immediately be seen by a physician. If the injury is only to the PCL and no other structures are involved, surgery can usually be avoided.

Meniscal Tears

Any shearing or twisting of the knee beyond its normal range of motion can damage the medial or lateral meniscus. Common scenarios are the same ones that cause sprains and ruptures of the ACL and include planting the foot with the toes pointed outward while twisting the upper body inward, and being tackled or hit on the outside of the leg or knee. Often, there's a combination of twisting and impact. As the meniscus ages, it can get brittle and may crack with minor trauma or simple repetitive use. Pain and swelling occur on the inner part of the knee; the pain is most noticeable when the knee is bent. People with torn menisci can develop something known as a *trick knee*, in which the joint peridically locks or catches as a result of a torn edge of the cartilage getting caught in the hinges of the joint.

Where the meniscus is concerned, an accurate and detailed diagnosis is especially important, because the cartilage won't heal well on its own and can't be replaced (though there has been incremental progress in developing synthetic substitutes). If the tear is clean rather than jagged and uneven, and if it occurs along the outer edge, close to a blood supply, then an orthopedic surgeon can very likely perform a meniscal repair. The advantage of this surgery is that you retain your entire shock-absorbing meniscus; however, the rehabilitation time following surgery can be up to six months. If the meniscus cannot be repaired, then a partial menisectomy will likely be performed. Only the torn part of the meniscus is removed, and as much intact meniscus as possible is left in the joint to maximize the remaining shock-absorbing capabilities of the knee. In cases where a major portion of the meniscus is damaged or removed, low-impact activites are recommended for exercise.

KJ CLOSEUP: Common Knee Injuries at a Glance

- Ligament sprains: Occur most frequently to the anterior cruciate ligament, or ACL.

- Patellar tendinitis: Inflammation of the tendon just below the kneecap, where it connects to the lower leg.

- Patellofemoral pain syndrome: Pain beneath the kneecap, caused by a number of factors.

- Meniscal tears: Damage to the special shock-absorbing pads that cushion the space between the thigh bone and the lower leg bone.

Patellar Tendinitis (Jumper's Knee)

Inflammation of the thick tendon that runs under the kneecap, connecting the quadriceps to the lower leg, is called *patellar tendinitis*. Heavy squatting, jumping, and sprinting all place a lot of stress on the patellar tendon and can cause a series of small tears along the tissue—and ultimately a partial or (in rare cases) complete rupture. The damage usually begins before symptoms are felt and results from the knee not having enough time to recover between bouts of exercise and activity. The pain is usually felt just below the kneecap, right on the tendon.

Since this is primarily an overuse condition resulting in inflammation, rest from aggravating activity is vital. Once the pain has subsided, a gradual return to your regular activities should be accompanied by stretching and strengthening exercises, such as partial squats.

Bursitis of the Knee

Bursitis of the knee is also known as *water on the knee*. The prepatellar bursa, a fluid-filled sac located right over the kneecap, becomes inflamed, causing pain, swelling, and a feeling of radiating heat around the joint. Knee bursitis can be precipitated by one incident—such as landing or falling on the knee—or can result from cumulative, hard impacts from running or jumping.

Rest, ice, and elevation help speed healing. If the pain is intense, a doctor can drain the bursa and relieve the irritation with a cortisone injection.

11

The Athletic Thigh

A great deal of the body's athletic power is produced in the upper leg, generating primarily from the quadriceps muscles, which act to extend the knee. The quads are responsible not just for motion, but also for stability. When you're standing still or walking, they provide the counterforce that keeps your leg from collapsing.

The thigh bone, or *femur*, is strong as well. Thick and cylindrical, it's the longest bone in the body, running from hip to knee, and endures an incredible amount of stress, actually bending quite a bit in the process. As hardy as it is, it can be a site of stress fractures among athletes. If you get into a semisquat position, knees slightly bent and hips flexed with your torso erect, you can feel the muscles of your thigh strain. Imagine landing or jumping from that position—generating 8 or 10 times your body weight—and you get an idea of the forces the femur is subject to.

Structures of the Thigh

Following are the important structures of the thigh.

Quadriceps

Once thought to consist of four muscles, we now know that the quadriceps actually contain five muscles: *rectus femoris*, which lies at the very front of the thigh and acts at both the knee and the hip; and *vastus intermedius, vastus lateralis, vastus medialis longus,* and *vastus medialis oblique.* The quads culminate in a single tendon that runs over the patella and attaches to the lower leg. Vastus medialis oblique and vastus lateralis have the important role of keeping the patella in proper alignment, one pulling the kneecap laterally toward the outer part of the knee, and the other pulling it in toward the body's midline.

Sartorius

The longest muscle in the human body, the *sartorius* starts by the hip joint and travels diagonally across the front of the thigh, attaching on the inside just below the knee joint.

Tensor Fascia Latae

A hip muscle, *tensor fascia lata* functions as a sling that pulls on the femur, helping to steady the trunk on the femur.

Iliotibial Band

The *iliotibial band* is a thick band of connective tissue that begins at the pelvis, crosses the hip, and inserts below the knee joint, crossing over its outer edge. You can feel it most prominently when the knee is slightly bent.

Hamstrings

The *hamstrings* are a group of three muscles that run parallel to each other up and down the back of the thigh. They include the *biceps femoris* (which has a short and a long head) on the lateral side, and *semitendinosus* and *semimembranosus* on the medial side. The upper portion of each attaches on the pelvis, just below your buttocks on your sitting bone (the sitting bone is known as the ischial tuberosity and is located at the lower end of the pelvic bone). The lower portions of the medial hamstrings attach to the inner portion of the tibia. The biceps femoris attaches on the outside to the fibula, just below the knee joint. Those two cablelike tendons you feel behind your knee are part of the hamstrings. The hamstrings are biarticular flexing the knee and extending the hip. When you bend forward, the hamstrings work (along with the muscles of the lower back) like strings of a marionette to

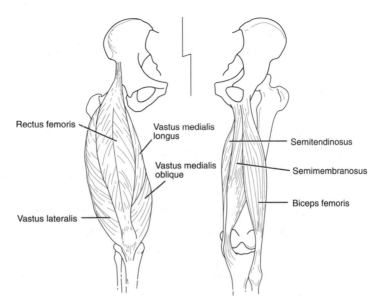

Anterior (front) view of the thigh: the quadriceps muscles

Posterior (rear) view of the thigh: the hamstring muscles

control your trunk and raise it back up to a vertical position. The hamstrings also tighten eccentrically when you run or walk to decelerate the swing of the lower leg so that the knee joint doesn't snap each time it extends.

The hamstrings have tendons that extend quite a distance into the belly of the muscle tissue. Since strains frequently occur at the junction between the muscle tissue and the tendon, the hamstrings may be at higher risk for this type of injury.

Biarticular muscles like the hamstrings tend to be more prone to injury if they perform different functions at each joint. If you're sprinting, for example, your body may require the hamstrings to forcefully contract to extend the hip, propelling the body forward at the same time that these muscles are stretched over the knee joint.

KJ TIP: Hamstrings Exercises

Trainers and coaches recommend a variety of exercises for strengthening the injury-prone hamstrings, which are often underconditioned and overstressed.

- *Hip extension:* This exercise can be done either on a multihip machine (a machine that allows you to adjust it to perform a variety of hip motions) or using a cable pulley coupled with an ankle strap in the gym. When performing hip extension, be sure to keep your trunk perfectly upright.
- *Hamstring curl:* When using the leg curl machine, adjust the pad so that it rests just above, and not on, the Achilles tendon. Choose light weights at first, increasing the poundage gradually. Lower and raise the weight slowly, pausing at full extension and full flexion. Don't bounce the weight, and don't arch your body.
- *Backward walking:* Walking or jogging backward on a track (being careful, of course, of obstructions and other people) can strengthen the hamstrings.
- *Reverse motion on an elliptical exerciser:* Elliptical exercisers are a cross between stairclimbers and treadmills; the motion is akin to cross-country skiing. The better models allow you to pedal your feet in a reverse motion, thus strengthening the hamstrings and gluteal muscles. Build up to doing the exercise with the ramp setting at low (in other words, no incline) and the resistance at high; and maintain a light pace (20 to 50 strides per minute).

Common Thigh Problems

Even though the muscles of the upper leg and the bone beneath them are among the strongest structures of the body, they are also subject to great amounts of stress.

Contusions

Because of their huge bulk in an exposed area of the body, the quads (in particular the rectus femoris) are susceptible to contusions, or direct blows. These are most likely to occur when another individual or an object bangs against the thigh while it's contracted. Contusions tear the muscle fibers, which leak fluid into the surrounding area, causing a pooling of blood known as a *hematoma* (or, more commonly, a bruise). If the bruise is particularly deep, scar tissue that forms within the injured muscle can calcify. The resulting condition, known as *myositis ossificans*, can be both painful and disabling.

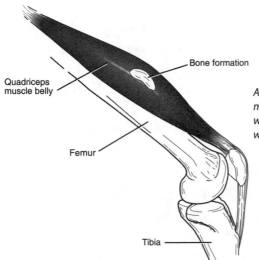

Quadriceps
muscle belly

Bone formation

Femur

Tibia

A contusion to the thigh can cause myositis ossificans, a condition in which there is a formation of bone within the belly of a muscle.

Immediate RICE is recommended. Keep the compression constant, and ice at least twice a day for the first 48 hours, 15 to 20 minutes each time. That will minimize not just the swelling, but also the likelihood that myositis ossificans will occur. For the first two days, avoid doing anything that stimulates blood flow to the area, including using massage or heat. After the first two days, motion is encouraged. The muscle injury itself will heal on its own in about three weeks, longer if the damage was extensive. If the pain is considerable, it's certainly worth seeing a sports healthcare professional. The important thing is to ensure that the scar tissue that develops as a natural part of the healing process doesn't form in a way that will inhibit your movement. If myositis ossificans has formed, extended rehabilitation may be necessary. Properly diagnosed by a physician, the condition can be monitored with x-rays so that you can be counseled regarding your return to activities.

Iliotibial Band Friction Syndrome

Iliotibial band friction syndrome is inflammation of the iliotibial band (ITB) or of the bursa located between the ITB and the lower end of the femur. The ITB's function as a knee stabilizer involves its sliding over the lateral surface of the knee joint (about 3,000 times for each mile you jog) as it bends and straightens. Overuse, poor biomechanics, or lack of specific stretching can cause the band to become tight and less resilient, squeezing the bursa and causing irritation. The condition is most common among distance cyclists and runners and may be especially aggravated by downhill running. The pain is localized over the outer portion of the knee. In rare cases, it hurts over the hip joint (the ITB slides over the bone in that area as well). Another common sensation is a creaking feeling on the lateral aspect of the knee joint.

Among the potential causes of ITB friction syndrome are:

- *Tightness of the ITB:* Test yourself for tightness of the ITB by lying on your side, with the leg you are testing on top. Bend your knee to a 90-degree angle. Bring your thigh in line with your trunk. Your thigh should easily drop down toward the other thigh. If it does not drop down, or you feel considerable tension on the outside of your thigh as you bring it down, then your ITB is tight.
- *Overpronation:* Overpronation increases the rotation of the lower leg, tightening the ITB and creating more friction between it and the bone.
- *Slanted roads:* Most paved roads are slanted for drainage at the edge of the road, creating a false discrepancy in the length of one leg compared to the other if running is in the same direction for extended periods of time.
- *Leg-length discrepancy:* ITB friction syndrome tends to afflict the shorter leg; as little as a one-quarter-inch difference can create biomechanical problems.
- *Overuse:* Running longer than you're used to, or running downhill when you're not used to it, can lead to ITB friction syndrome.

To treat ITB friction syndrome, ice the knee twice a day. If the pain is chronic, rest from the offensive activity for two weeks. During this time, cross-train with activities that do not cause pain, and begin very mild stretching exercises for the ITB. When the acute phase subsides, begin incorporating ITB crossover stretches as part of your exercise routine, particularly after your warm-up and after your workout. Other measures that may reduce strain on the ITB:

- Place a heel pad on the lateral side of the heel.
- If you overpronate, experiment with a semirigid arch support.

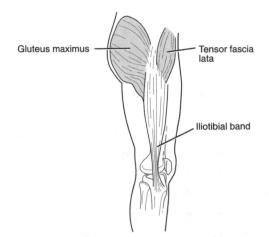

Gluteus maximus

Tensor fascia lata

Iliotibial band

The iliotibial band serves as the attachment of a number of hip muscles. Stress, overuse, and tightness can cause it to rub or snap over the bursae located near the knee or hip, causing pain and inflammation.

- If you're a cyclist, you can experiment with shifting seat height and toe position. In general, toeing outward will take pressure off the ITB, as will raising the seatpost or moving it farther back.

Hamstring Tendinitis

Hamstring tendinitis is inflammation of the hamstring tendons, most commonly at the points where the muscles become tendons. Since the proximal tendons of this muscle group extend relatively far down the back of the thigh, and the distal tendons extend a good distance up the back of the thigh, the pain caused by hamstring tendinitis can be felt in the midthigh even though the injury is not in the muscle belly. Overuse and lack of warm-up are the common causes. The condition has a high tendency of recurrence—25 percent among athletes in one study. Two characteristics researchers have noticed among people susceptible to hamstring injuries:

1. A stark imbalance between strength of the quads and the hamstrings. To some degree, that imbalance is normal because the quads are intrinsically stronger. When hamstring strength is less than 60 percent as stong as the quadricep muscle in the front of the leg, there is an increased susceptibility to strains and pulls of the hamstring.
2. A discrepancy in strength between the left and right legs. If one leg is more than 10 percent stronger than the other, there is a higher incidence of hamstring injury.

For acute injuries, immediately begin RICE; compression is especially important to minimize swelling and inflammation. For chronic injuries: since muscle imbalance is associated with hamstring injuries, it's important to stretch and strengthen the backs and fronts of both legs. Stretching should only be done after warming up the muscle and should never be painful or uncomfortable. Stretching is important not only in increasing the flexibility of the muscle, but it is thought to help the scar tissue that forms as part of the healing process to line up with the muscle and tendon fibers. Overzealous stretching can do more harm than good, tearing the fibers further. Eccentric exercise is particularly important, because it strengthens the muscle in a functional way, the way it is usually used for activity. For example, when doing leg curls, lower the weight slowly and evenly against resistance for best results.

For chronic tendinitis, ice is important after activity to decrease the inflammation. You may want to try taking over-the-counter NSAIDs for 7 to 10 days. Try reducing activities that aggravate the situation, and wear an elastic bandage or Neoprene sleeve.

Allow for complete healing—10 days to three weeks for a minor injury, and up to six months for a severe or chronic injury. Cycling and stair-climbing are good alternative exercises that don't stress the hamstrings. Once the pain is gone, gradually reintroduce exercises. Warm up and stretch. Don't play when you're tired: the fact that most hamstring injuries occur early in the game or late in the game indicates that you may be better protected if your body is limber before you step onto the field or begin a hard workout.

KJ TIP: Preventing Recurrent Hamstring Pain and Injury
Here are three measures you can take to minimize the odds of recurrent hamstring tendinitis:

1. Incorporate light stretching and strengthening exercises, even if you're only capable of limited motions. Go up to, but never beyond, the point of pain. Return to exercise should be gradual. Use pain as your guide. Increase your activity by no more than 10 percent per week as you make your comeback from injury.

2. Transverse friction massage performed by a certified sports therapist may help prevent recurrence by helping the scar tissue that is forming as a result of the healing process to align with the muscle and tendon fibers.

3. Some studies indicate that a 10-day course of ultrasound administered by a physical therapist can also influence the scar tissue to align with the muscle and tendon fibers.

Greater Trochanteric Bursitis

Inflammation of the bursa on the outside of the hip area is called *greater trochanteric bursitis*. This injury can cause nagging hip pain on the outer upper part of the thigh. It can be caused by a number factors, including a leg-length discrepancy, tightness of the ITB, weakness of the muscles that abduct the hip (these muscles also stabilize the trunk when your weight is supported on only one leg), and running on a banked road or track.

Treat the inflammation first—ice, take NSAIDs, and rest from the offensive activity. After the acute pain has subsided, be sure to include stretches for the ITB and strengthening for the hip abductors in your exercise routine. In addition, you may want to find out if you have a significant leg-length discrepancy requiring a heel lift.

Stress Fracture of the Femur

Microscopic cracks in the shaft (the long part of the bone), neck (the area connecting the shaft to the head), or head (the ball part of the ball-and-socket hip joint) of the femur can be caused by overuse and overstress. As thick as the femur is, it is the conduit for transferring and absorbing large amounts of force between the upper and lower extremities: 10 to 20 times body weight when engaged in sports activities. If the fracture is in the head or neck, you may experience diffuse pain when active, either in the area of the groin or along the front of the thigh. At rest, there is no discomfort. Stress fractures along the shaft are more difficult to spot; sometimes the pain is only evident when there is direct bending pressure along the front of the leg, over the area of injury.

If a stress fracture is diagnosed at the femoral head or neck, careful diagnosis is necessary in order to make sure that the situation doesn't progress to a complete fracture, which could threaten the blood supply to the femur and cause a displaced fracture, necessitating surgery. In the vast majority of cases, however, reduction of activities for two months allows the situation to resolve itself. In the interim, light cycling and swimming can be used to maintain aerobic fitness.

After recovery, stretching and strengthening exercises targeting the front and rear muscles of the thigh and hip are important to prevent the muscular fatigue and imbalance that sometimes precipitate stress fractures.

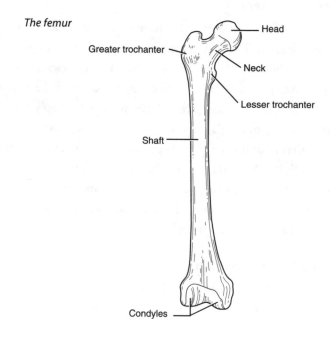

The femur

Greater trochanter

Head

Neck

Lesser trochanter

Shaft

Condyles

12

The Athletic Back

Perhaps more than any other body structure, the back requires a combination of conditioning, flexibility, and biomechanical efficiency to maintain its integrity and stability for a lifetime of performance.

The spinal column is a stack of individual bones (*vertebrae*) separated by spongy pads known as *intervertebral discs*, or more commonly, just *discs*. It provides the framework to which the large muscles of your back attach and houses and protects the long canal of nerves (the *spinal cord*) that transport sensory and motor messages between your body and your brain.

The spine is not a perfectly straight column, but rather it has an S-shaped curvature to it. There is an inward curve up by your neck (the *cervical* region of your spine), an outward curve in your upper back (the *thoracic* region), and another inward curve in your low back (the *lumbar* region). When these normal curves are maintained, the position is referred to as a *neutral spine*, and the stresses placed on your spinal column can be appropriately dispersed.

The lumbar spine, or lower back, bears a great deal of stress both from the frequent impact of the lower extremities and from the twisting and maneuvering of the upper extremities; as a result, it is very susceptible to injury. Back pain afflicts 80 percent of all Americans at some point in their lives and is one of the most frequent reasons for visits to the doctor's office and days missed from work.

Because of this toll, back pain is one of the most studied areas in medical research. Yet it remains mysterious; once injured, the lower back can cause a protracted episode of chronic pain. And, because of the network of nerves running through the spinal canal, an injury or tissue damage can cause pain that radiates to far-flung areas of the body, shooting down past the buttocks, thigh, and even into the foot. In some cases, the source of the pain can be physically pinpointed. But in others, it remains a mystery. Indeed, it has become evident to orthopedists that all of the high-tech diagnostic images used in attempting to find the source of back pain in an individual can be quite misleading. People with very disabling back pain can have diagnostic tests that are perfectly normal. In contrast, abnormalities can be seen in the diagnostic imaging procedures of people with no back-pain symptoms whatsoever. Far more conclusive and helpful is a low-tech approach. If you suffer from back pain, you'd be much better off with a physician who gleaned information from a hands-on examination rather than an MRI or CT scan alone.

For treatment, the low-tech approach is, once again, generally much more effective. Nine-tenths of all mechanical back pain goes away on its own, helped along by such conservative measures as light stretching, over-the-counter pain medication, and adequate rest from offensive activities. Newly touted laser procedures have become far overused and are often ineffective. They work in only a small percentage of cases.

Structures of the Back

Vertebrae

Vertebrae are the bones that make up the spine. There are seven in the cervical region (each bone is labeled, C1 through C7), which are involved in the movement of your neck. These are the smallest bones of the spine because they have the least amount of weight to bear, but they are also the most prone to severe traumatic injury.

The central 12 vertebrae (T1 through T12) make up the thoracic region of the spine. They are not involved in movement to the extent that the upper and lower regions of the spine are; rather they serve the function, along with the ribs, of creating a cavity—the thoracic cavity—to support and protect the heart and lungs.

The next five vertebrae (L1 through L5) are the thickest, but also the most prone to stress injuries because they bear the brunt of weight from above and force from below. The *sacrum* is a series of five fused vertebrae that sit just below the lumbar spine. The space between the lowest lumbar vertebra and the sacral vertebrae is the most mobile part of the lower spine, and the most prone to injury. Below the sacrum is the *coccyx*, or tailbone, which is the very base of the spine.

Each vertebra has a solid portion (called the body) toward the front of the body and a ring of bone that extends toward the rear of the body. It is this ring of bone that houses the spinal cord in a cavity called the *spinal canal.*

The areas where vertebrae come in contact with each other are known as *facet joints.* These are joints, just like the other major joints of your body. They have articular cartilage, ligaments, and a joint capsule.

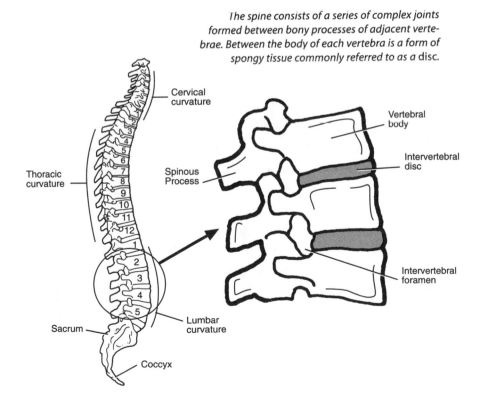

The spine consists of a series of complex joints formed between bony processes of adjacent vertebrae. Between the body of each vertebra is a form of spongy tissue commonly referred to as a disc.

Cervical curvature

Thoracic curvature

Spinous Process

Sacrum

Lumbar curvature

Coccyx

Vertebral body

Intervertebral disc

Intervertebral foramen

Intervertebral Discs

Each *intervertebral disc* is made of fibrocartilage, and each sits between the vertebrae. These discs make up about 25 percent of the length of the spinal column. The discs act as shock absorbers, and they allow the spine to flex and extend. The structure of each disc can be compared to a jelly donut—there is a center of semifluid material (*nucleus pulposus*) that is surrounded by a strong ring of fibrocartilage (*annulus fibrosus*). When you bend forward, the front of the jelly donut (disc) is compressed, and the jelly (nucleus pulposus) is pushed backward. When you bend backward the process is reversed.

Longitudinal Ligaments

Longitudinal ligaments are strong ligaments that stabilize the bones of the spine, preventing excessive bending and rotation.

Erector Spinae

The primary trunk muscles for bending backward (extending) at the waist are known as the *erector spinae* group. This layered series of muscles includes the *iliocostalis*, *longissimus*, and *spinalis* muscles.

Rectus abdominis

Rectus abdominis is the primary trunk muscle for flexing, or bending forward, at the waist.

Internal and External Obliques

These *internal oblique* and *external oblique* muscles of the abdomen, when they work simultaneously, aid the rectus abdominis in flexing the trunk. When they act individually, they rotate or bend the trunk to the side.

KJ FACT: Diagnosing the Cause of Back Pain

Despite the advent of high-tech imaging equipment, the most essential tools to diagnosing back pain remain the taking of a thorough medical history, and a hands-on exam by a specialist. In many cases, the supposed abnormalities detected by such things as x-rays and MRIs are unrelated to any back pain a patient may report.

Common Back Problems

The incidence of back problems increases sharply with age, but a little knowledge can go a long way toward avoiding and addressing such injuries.

Herniated Disc

Recall that the intervertebral discs are filled with a gel-like material called the nucleus pulposus. When you bend forward or backward, one side of the vertebrae compress against each other, squeezing the discs and pushing the nucleus pulposus in each disc toward the opposite side. As long as the fibrous capsule enveloping the fluid remains intact, the system functions adequately. But an acute injury—such as twisting the spine or suddenly compressing it under a heavy weight—can damage the fibrous ring (annulus fibrosus) that contains the nucleus. This also occurs with wear and tear or overuse. Also, aging can decrease the fluid content of the discs.

In all of these cases, the result can be what is known as a *herniated disc* (the term *slipped disc* is often used, but it's not accurate). When a disc is damaged, the annulus fibrosus is weakened and may develop microtears. As a result, the nucleus pulposus bulges out of its confined space. If the weakened area is near the rear of the disk (which it almost always is, because we stress this area by bending forward so much), pressure may be put on the *nerve root*, the part of the nerve that branches off the spinal cord. When you perform activities that push the nucleus pulposus toward the area of injured cartilage rings, you may feel pain locally due to inflammation, or you may

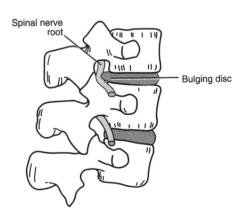

Spinal nerve root

Bulging disc

When a disc "slips," or herniates, its soft tissue bulges out and may press against a nerve root.

feel pain that radiates to other parts of your body that follow the pathway of that nerve. The more irritated the nerve root is, the farther along the pathway of the nerve you will feel the pain.

Discs are not usually injured from one traumatic episode, but rather from many small episodes. Every time you bend forward with your back unsupported and every time you sit slumped in your chair, you are squeezing the front of the disc and pushing the nucleus pulposus toward the back of the disc. Over time, the rings of cartilage weaken, but you still may not feel pain. Then one day you do something totally ordinary like bend over to tie your shoe, and the effect is like the straw that broke the camel's back—the disc bulges.

If the annulus fibrosus is not broken, only stretched, the bulge is called a *protruded disc*. If the sheath is indeed broken, but the disc material hasn't penetrated a second boundary formed by the posterior longitudinal ligament running along the spinal canal, the condition is diagnosed as an *extruded disc*. But if the disc has broken beyond this layer as well, then a fragment may actually float freely within the spinal canal, a condition known as a *sequestrated disc*.

The overwhelming majority of bulging discs occur in the lumbar region, an area that is under a lot of stress when you bend forward and sit. When you sit, unless you maintain the natural inward curve of your low back, the discs experience stress similar to bending forward. The nerves in the lumbar region (the *femoral nerve* and the *sciatic nerve*) run to the buttocks, thigh, and lower leg (hence the term *sciatica* to describe pain, tingling, or limb weakness that shoots down the leg). If you stand, walk, or lie down (particularly with your feet flat and your knees bent), the compression is often lessened and the pain may be relieved.

In 90 percent of all cases, conservative measures—rest, heat or ice, and an anti-inflammatory drug such as ibuprofen—will allow the disc and nerve inflammation to heal on its own. *Rest* does not mean bed rest. It has been shown that people with disc injuries who rest in bed longer than two days take longer to get better than people who don't.

Since inflammation is present, things that increase your circulation, such as activity, will speed up the process. Just be careful that the activity you choose is not stressful to your back. Bending forward and sitting are among the things most stressful to your discs.

It's important during the healing time—a period that can take two to six weeks—to refrain from lifting heavy objects and performing activities that can reinjure the area. Once healing is more than 75 percent complete, gradually introduce an exercise program geared at strengthening the muscles of the back, abdomen, and lower extremities, thus reducing the possibility of a recurrence. All of the exercise you do should be with your spine held in the neutral position, with the three normal curves of the spine intact. When you do have to lift things, take care to do so with good mechanics— use the strong muscles of your legs. In extreme cases, surgery or an arthroscopic procedure can reduce the bulged disc or even fuse the injured vertebra to the adjacent one, thus relieving pressure on the nerve root.

Cervical Disc Injury

Inflammation of the intervertebral discs and possibly the adjacent nerve roots in the cervical spine can be caused by degeneration or injury of the discs. This condition may cause pain along the pathway of the nerves that run into the upper extremities.

Facet Joint Syndrome

Some cases of chronic low-back pain may be caused by degeneration of the articular cartilage of the facet joints, the joints that connect the vertebrae. As a result, they can grind against each other, causing the formation of bony spikes that press against the nerves from the spinal cord. As in the case of a herniated disc, the pain can be felt in the area of the injury, or anywhere along the pathway of the irritated nerve. In this case, extending your spine backward may be irritating, as that is the position that compresses the facet joints.

Muscle Strain

As distinguished from spinal pain, muscle pain is more likely to feel localized, and is more sensitive to touch. The pain doesn't radiate as it would with disc herniation. Acute muscle pain of the back, like muscle pain elsewhere in the body, responds well to ice during the first 48 hours.

Spondylosis

Spondylosis is a condition in which a vertebra is misshapen, either congenitally or as a result of a stress fracture. The vertebra can then slip forward on the vertebra just below it, a condition known as *spondylolisthesis*. Spondylosis can be detected on x-ray. Some cases are extremely unstable and require surgery to stabilize them.

KJ TIP: Low-Back Pain Overview

• For the first weeks following injury, follow conservative therapy measures—over-the-counter NSAIDS, rest, gentle stretching, and the application of heat.

• Avoid too much rest—lack of movement, in most cases, will contribute to back pain. Remember, activity increases circulation, which will decrease inflammation.

• Do low-impact aerobic activities and light stretching and strengthening exercises that target the lower back and abdomen.

• Consult a physician if you experience any of the following:

  * Pain that does not subside after six weeks

  * Numbness and tingling, or muscle weakness

  * Bowel or bladder problems

  * Night pain

13

The Athletic Shoulder

When we talk about the shoulder from the perspective of anatomy, we're actually referring to a skeletal cage (or girdle) that consists of four separate joints—the *sternoclavicular, acromioclavicular, glenohumeral,* and *scapulothoracic* joints. But when you refer to the shoulder in colloquial terms, you're actually talking about the *glenohumeral joint,* the ball-and-socket joint located where your upper arm (the *humerus*) meets a cavity on the side of your shoulder blade known as the *glenoid fossa.* This is the most mobile of all joints in the body, allowing you the freedom to use your shoulder to place your hand almost anywhere to perform activities as broad and powerful as swinging a club, and as fine as the manipulation of a timepiece. In order to manage this range, however, the shoulder's design is inherently unstable. It's described as a ball-and-socket joint, but it's more like a golf ball sitting on a tee—the top of your humerus sits on the shallow saucerlike cavity, the glenoid fossa. Without the muscles, tendons, ligaments, and joint capsule all serving as a sling to hold the unit together, the shoulder joint would unravel.

There are certain movements during which your shoulder is particularly unstable. If you experiment with moving your shoulder, you'll see that lifting it above 90 degrees in the plane out toward the side of your body (abduction) feels unstable. That instability isn't troublesome for routine activities such as reaching for something in a cupboard. However, when you compound that relatively unstable position with the stress that accompanies overhead athletic movements such as pitching a baseball, striking overhead with a tennis racket, or lifting your body weight while rock climbing, the possibility of injury greatly increases. The muscles most responsible for shoulder stability are the four muscle–tendon structures that comprise the shoulder's rotator cuff. These muscles include the *supraspinatus, infraspinatus, teres minor,* and *subscapularis.*

Since the soft tissue of the shoulder joint is much more responsible for stability than that of other joints that can rely predominantly on their bony stability, the solution to preventing injuries is to maintain a balance of strength and flexibility in all of the muscles of the shoulder. And these include the chest muscles (*pectoralis major* and *pectoralis minor*); the scapular (shoulderblade) muscles (*trapezius, levator scapulae, rhomboids,* and *serratus anterior*); the *deltoids*; the rotator cuff muscles; the *latissimus dorsi*; and the muscles of the upper arm (*biceps and triceps*).

Structures of the Shoulder

Glenohumeral Joint

The shoulder proper, *the glenohumeral joint* attaches the humerus to the glenoid fossa (cavity) of your scapula (shoulder blade). While the cavity is shallow, a fibrocartilage disc known as the *glenoid labrum* forms a rim around it deepening the socket and providing a more secure (though not foolproof) fit.

Sternoclavicular Joint

The *sternoclavicular joint* attaches your sternum to your collarbone, or *clavicle,* allowing for the small amount of rotation of the bones necessary when you lift your arm overhead.

Acromioclavicular Joint

The *acromioclavicular joint* is on the edge of your shoulder, where the clavicle meets a part of the shoulder blade called the *acromion.*

Scapulothoracic Joint

The *scapulothoracic joint* is not a true synovial joint, but rather the attachment (by muscles) of your shoulder blade to your trunk.

Trapezius

Most prominent along the slope between your neck and shoulder, the *trapezius* is a broad, flat muscle with three parts (upper, middle, lower). The muscle extends all the way down to the center of the back. It controls motion of the scapula during activities that require overhead motions, such as swimming and tennis.

Rhomboids

These muscles attach the scapula to the spine. They are important in controlling the position of the scapula, retracting it or pulling it back toward the spine during shoulder activities.

Serratus Anterior

This muscle goes from the inner underside of the shoulder blade, around to the front of the trunk, and attaches to the ribs in nine spots. It protracts

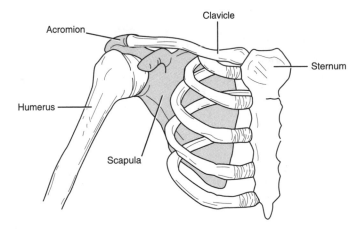

The four joints of the shoulder are formed where two bones come together—except in the case of the scapulothoracic joint, which is formed by the attachment of the scapula to the trunk by muscles.

(pulls) the scapula forward and helps to tip it upward to position for overhead movements.

Rotator Cuff

The *rotator cuff* is a mass of four muscles and their tendons that move and stabilize the head of the humerus in the glenoid fossa. In other words, they keep the ball in the socket as you raise, lower, and lift your arm through various arcs and angles around the joint. The cuff includes the supraspinatus, the subscapularis, the teres minor, and the infraspinatus, all of which blend into a single tendon.

Deltoids

These muscles, which position the shoulder, cover the joint like epaulets. There are three aspects to the muscle (anterior, middle, and posterior), one each for lifting the arm forward, out to the side, and backward.

Pectoralis Major

The *pectoralis major* is the larger chest muscle, which is used in throwing and pushing. Strength of this muscle is directly associated with power and speed of throwing and pushing movements.

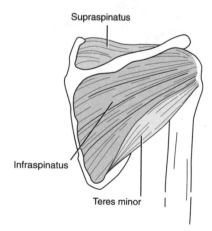

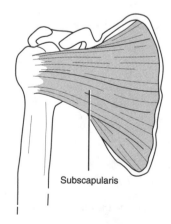

Posterior (rear) view of the rotator cuff muscles

Anterior (front) view of the rotator cuff muscles

> **KJ FACT: Shoulder Power**
> A pitcher who wants to increase the speed of his pitches can do so by strengthening the pectoralis major and latissimus dorsi muscles.

Latissimus Dorsi

The major muscle of the back, the *latissimus dorsi* looks like a vest that covers almost the entire back. It is the muscle you use to pull yourself up when climbing. It's also used in pulling, swimming, rowing, and in swinging or throwing motions.

Biceps Brachii

This muscle has two heads: the short head, which crosses only the elbow, and the long head, which functions at both the shoulder and the elbow. The long head of the biceps helps stabilize the shoulder joint and may become more important in shoulders with a weak or torn rotator cuff.

Triceps Brachii

Located in the back of the upper arm, the triceps is involved in throwing and pushing motions that move the arm downward and backward, as when you're pushing back on the poles during skiing, or in the pull-through phase of a freestyle swim stroke.

Subacromial Bursa

The *subacromial bursa* is a watery sac that allows the tendons of the rotator cuff to ride smoothly over bone within the shoulder joint.

Glenoid Labrum

The *glenoid labrum* is a rim of fibrocartilage that surrounds the glenoid fossa, deepening the socket and imparting some extra stability to the joint.

Joint Capsule

This fibrous capsule surrounding the glenohumeral joint is thin and, in a normal shoulder, remarkably loose. It is this looseness that contributes to the joint's tremendous mobility.

Glenohumeral Ligaments

These three ligaments strengthen the front of the joint capsule. They appear as thickenings of the joint capsule itself, rather than clearly distinct structures. If these ligaments become stretched out, a subluxation or dislocation of the joint may occur.

Common Shoulder Problems

A full range of motion and poor stability characterize the shoulder and explain why athletic stresses take a heavy toll on the soft tissue of your shoulder. Careful warm-ups, stretches, and strengthening exercises are essential preventative measures against injury.

Impingement Syndrome (Rotator Cuff Tendinitis and Bursitis)

Impingement syndrome is marked by inflammation of one or more of the four rotator cuff tendons that run through a tiny space between the bony tip of your shoulder (the *acromion process*) and the ball-and-socket joint directly beneath it. The condition, which is extremely common, affects primarily those involved in activities requiring repetitive overhead movements, including weightlifting, swimming, and volleyball. Impingement syndrome starts out insidiously. One of the rotator cuff tendons, usually the supraspinatus, becomes slightly inflamed; as a result, it swells a little bit, crowding the already tight subacromial space, a small space between the acromion at the tip of your shoulder and the ball at the top of the humerus. That space also houses the *subacromial bursa*, a water-filled pad designed to reduce friction between the tendons and bones in the area.

Once even the tiniest amount of inflammation begins, both the bursa and the tendon become involved in a vicious cycle in which continued movement further inflames the soft tissue. Eventually, the space becomes so tight with swollen tissue that the tendon may tear. If the deterioration is allowed to continue, it can lead to a complete rupture of the rotator cuff, causing inability to smoothly move the shoulder joint and often making it impossible to raise your arm at all. If you are an overhead throwing athlete, such as a pitcher, tendinitis of the rotator cuff may have a different cause.

Impingement problems are usually progressive; they start out as small, intermittent, nagging pains, and eventually progress to a full-fledged rup-

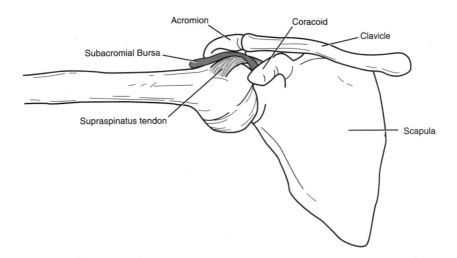

Shoulder impingement syndrome occurs when the supraspinatus tendon and/or subacromial bursa—both running through the tight space known as the coraco-acromial arch—become inflamed.

ture. If you notice the beginnings of pain from deep inside the edge of your shoulder in the form of creaking, snapping, or inflammation, pull back immediately from activities that exacerbate the pain. Rest the area until the inflammation subsides—you can still stretch lightly and exercise the shoulder within the range of motion that feels comfortable. For example, when the supraspinatus is inflamed, the pain is usually felt when your arm is raised to the side at an arc of 80 to 120 degrees. That means that you may still be able to achieve mobility beneath the horizontal plane—and you should, in order to keep some flexibility in the inflamed tendons. If the tendon is only minimally strained, it will heal on its own within four to six weeks. After that time, you can gradually resume your normal activities, adding stretching and strengthening exercises to condition and maintain the scapular and shoulder muscles and tendons. Anti-inflammatory medications and ice (applied after exercise) can help speed the healing process by reducing inflammation.

Calcific Tendinitis/Bursitis

As a result of injury, overuse, or simply age, calcium deposits form in the supraspinatus tendon and/or the subacromial bursa. The intense pain

Impingement syndrome of the suprapinatus, a rotator cuff tendon, usually causes pain when the arm is raised to the side higher than 90 degrees.

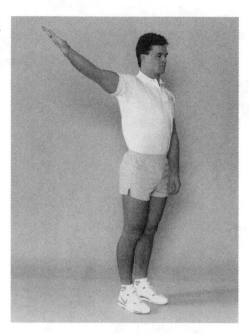

experienced along the top and front of the shoulder is relieved only when the elbow is held close to the body.

An injection of cortisone or a local anesthetic can relieve the acute pain. Anti-inflammatory drugs may be effective, too. In worst-case scenarios, surgery can remove the deposits; but to prevent them from recurring, a stretching and strengthening program is necessary.

Shoulder Separation

A shoulder separation is a sprain of the ligaments connecting the acromion to the clavicle. The acromioclavicular joint is composed of small bones, so it takes only a moderate impact against the outer edge of the shoulder—such as might happen when being slammed against a wall or when falling on the shoulder—for a separation of the bones to occur. The extent of damage varies; a separation can be minor and involve just a slight stretching of the ligaments, in which case it will be painful to raise your arm for a few days. Or the injury can involve complete rupture of the ligaments that hold the joint together, which causes swelling and intense pain—the shoulder will be discolored, and the separation may even be obvious to the eye.

Treatment depends on the severity of the injury. A minor separation may require only a couple of days to recover on its own; ice and NSAIDS can be of great help. Avoid overhead lifting during the healing phase. When completely healed, there may be a noticeable bump in the area of the injury because the ligaments are stretched out, causing one side of the joint to be higher than the other. This is a normal part of the healing process.

Shoulder Subluxation and Dislocation

A sharp impact against the arm while it's extended can cause the head of the humerus to pop out of the shoulder socket, stretching or tearing the gleno-humeral ligaments and joint capsule. If the bone pops right back in on its own, it's known as a subluxation, or partial dislocation. Subluxation of the shoulder can also be caused by a gradual stretching of the ligaments and joint capsule in the front of the shoulder, such as occurs during repetitive, extreme movements of the sort performed in baseball pitching.

This type of injury can usually be successfully treated through a proper strengthening program that targets the scapular and rotator cuff muscles. Subluxations cause acute pain at first, then the pain subsides—but may return several hours later. Subluxations can heal on their own with ice, rest, and strengthening exercises, but you still may consider consulting an orthopedist to make sure that the ligaments will heal properly; if they don't, you may be susceptible to recurrent episodes.

Complete dislocations are obvious in terms of the degree of pain, spasms, and the obvious misalignment of the bones. Since dislocations aren't overuse injuries, it's hard to take preventive measures, except to avoid falling on an outstretched arm (skiing and skating falls are common scenarios for these injuries). Dislocations demand immediate medical attention and should be iced en route to the emergency room.

Fractured Clavicle (Broken Collarbone)

One of the most common bicycle injuries, a clavicle fracture occurs when you fall on the top of the shoulder or an outstretched arm. You'll feel intense pain at the site of the fracture and have difficulty moving your arm. Ice and immobilize the injury on the way to the emergency room. The doctor will fit you with a sling or figure-eight shoulder harness, which is a specially designed sling that will hold the bone in place until it begins to fuse. Healing takes approximately six to eight weeks.

Adhesive Capsulitis (Frozen Shoulder)

Tightening and scarring of the joint capsule of the glenohumeral joint is called *adhesive capsulitis*. The capsule is pleated like an accordion, so that as the joint moves, the folds separate and expand. The shoulder capsule is peculiar, however, in that after an injury or a period of immobility (or sometimes for no known reason), the folds can adhere to each other, and the capsule thickens or shrinks, making movement painful and restricted.

To counter the condition, mobility of the shoulder may gradually be restored with the aid of physical therapy (the therapist will manipulate the joint through a prescribed range of motion) and frequent, light stretching exercises. Anti-inflammatory medication, ultrasound, and in some cases, a steroid injection can speed healing and reduce pain. In severe or persistent cases, an orthopedist can perform arthroscopy or manipulation under anesthesia to loosen the adhesions.

14

The Athletic Elbow

Three separate joints meet in the space commonly referred to as the elbow, all of them sharing a single joint capsule. That complexity is what allows you to bend and straighten your elbow and rotate your forearm (and thus your hand). This rotation is called supination and pronation, the same terms used to describe the side-to-side rotation of the foot controlled by the ankle joint. In the hand and arm, these movements are crucial to pushing, pulling, grabbing, and throwing.

Inside the elbow joint, the humerus and the bones of the lower arm (the *radius* and the *ulna*) not only hinge, but also rotate. In fact, the forearm bones actually cross over each other during pronation and supination.

Yet the elbow is a small joint; it is not meant to handle much stress. It's not well-padded, either, which poses an additional concern. Because the joint serves as a passageway for major arteries and nerves, a dislocation or fracture can have serious consequences to mobility, beyond mere damage to bones. There are important preventive measures you should take to protect your elbow during activity:

- *Use proper technique:* In all athletic motions—throwing, striking with a tennis racket, paddling, or rowing, for example—be sure to engage the large muscles of your trunk, hips, and legs. This takes the strain off the smaller elbow joint. If you don't know how to perform motions correctly, consult a coach or trainer who can teach you proper form.

- *Stretch and strengthen:* Follow the proper exercises for maintaining the muscles and tendons that control the elbow joint. Since many of them also move the shoulder and wrist, maintain a balanced conditioning program that includes all the muscles of the upper limbs.
- *Wear safety gear:* When involved in sports where balance is an issue, such as inline skating, wear pads that protect the elbows and the wrists. Many elbow injuries occur as a result of landing on an unprotected wrist.
- *Learn to fall properly:* For sports that put you at risk of falling, consult a coach or trainer about learning to fall properly—not on an outstretched hand, but by rolling backward over the scapula and then the shoulder (a maneuver known as the *shoulder roll*).

Structures of the Elbow

The multijoint elbow region is the centerpoint for much of the fine muscle coordination required in hand and arm movements.

Humeroulnar Joint

The *humeroulnar joint*, the elbow proper, is where the ulna of the forearm meets and hinges with the the base (*trochlea*) of the humerus. The ulna runs along the forearm on the same side as your littlest finger.

Humeroradial Joint

The *humeroradial joint* is the connecting point between the upper arm and the second bone of your forearm, the radius. These two bones attach at a point called the *capitellum*. (The radius runs along the thumb side of your forearm.)

Proximal Radioulnar Joint

The *proximal radioulnar joint* joins the two forearm bones at the end closest to the elbow.

Medial and Lateral Epicondyles

The *medial and lateral epicondyles* are the knobs at the lower end of the upper arm. The muscles that extend the wrist attach to the lateral epicondyle

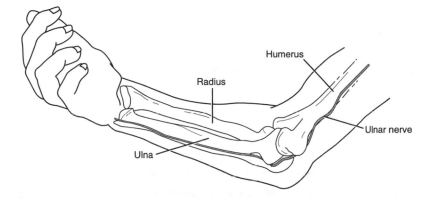

Humerus

Radius

Ulnar nerve

Ulna

The ulnar nerve, which runs close to the surface of the skin, presents a special risk in injuries to the elbow.

(that's the knob on the outer part of your elbow), and the muscles that flex the wrist attach to the medial epicondyle (the inner elbow knob).

Biceps Brachii

The major muscle of the front part of your upper arm, the *biceps* acts to bend your elbow. It has two heads: one that crosses both the shoulder and the elbow, and one that crosses just the elbow. The long head can act as a shoulder flexor as well as a flexor of the elbow.

Triceps Brachii

This three-part muscle is located at the back of the upper arm. It functions to extend or straighten the elbow.

Wrist Flexors

These muscles flex the wrist, or pull the palm of the hand toward the forearm. They are also capable of assisting the muscles of the upper arm with elbow flexion. These muscles cross the elbow and attach on the humerus at the medial epicondyle.

Wrist Extensors

These muscles extend the wrist, or lift the back of the hand up toward the forearm. They are also capable of assisting the muscles of the upper arm with elbow flexion. These muscles cross the elbow and attach on the humerus at the lateral epicondyle.

Ulnar (Medial) Collateral Ligament

Attaching the humerus to the ulna, the *ulnar (medial) collateral ligament* is a major contributor to the joint's stability.

Nerves of the Elbow

Nerves running through the elbow include the *ulnar, radial,* and *median* nerves. The ulnar nerve is vulnerable to injury at the elbow because of its superficial location. It runs right along the medial epicondyle. Striking this area, also known as the "funny bone," results in pain and tingling along the pathway of the nerve, down the forearm, and into the little finger.

Common Elbow Problems

In addition to injury from repetitive stress, the elbow is susceptible to trauma that can damage the nerves running through this sparsely padded region.

Epicondylitis

Epicondylitis is the name for inflammation of the tendons that attach the forearm muscles to the epicondyles. These muscles flex and extend the wrist and fingers.

One form of epicondylitis affects the lateral (outer) side of the elbow, the attachment site for muscles that extend your wrist. The condition is commonly called *tennis elbow* because it tends to affect racket-sports players, but it can also be a problem for golfers and individuals involved in repetitive use of the hands and wrists such as typing. The combination of tightly gripping a racket or golf club while simultaneously stressing the wrist extensors creates an overload that eventually causes inflammation of the tissue. Other movements can also trigger the condition, such as rowing or paddling. Here's one way to know if it's tennis elbow: you'll experience pain when simultaneously grasping and lifting something, such as a full cup of coffee, or when shaking hands.

The second form of epicondylitis, medial epicondylitis (that's pain and inflammation along the inner elbow knob), commonly affects golfers, therefore it is sometimes referred to as *golfer's elbow*. It also may affect pitchers and throwers.

The main cause of epicondylitis is usually overuse, sometimes coupled with poor technique. If you're playing tennis three times a week at a high level of intensity, but you're swinging with your arm and wrist alone rather than engaging the hips and shoulders, you'll eventually place too much stress on the muscles and tendons of your elbow and forearm. You may also be gripping the racket (or the oar handle, if you're a rower or paddler) too tightly; or the racket grip may be too wide for your fingers.

Rest from the aggravating activity. Either form of epicondylitis—lateral or medial—can linger and become chronic if you don't allow for proper healing. Use ice twice a day to reduce pain and inflammation. Perform mild stretching exercises frequently. Strengthening should be started when the pain dissipates. Wearing a brace or support in an attempt to bypass the inflammation won't do anything to prevent recurrence—it will only help once you've allowed the inflammation to completely subside. Chronic cases may require medical attention. An orthopedist may prescribe NSAIDs or a

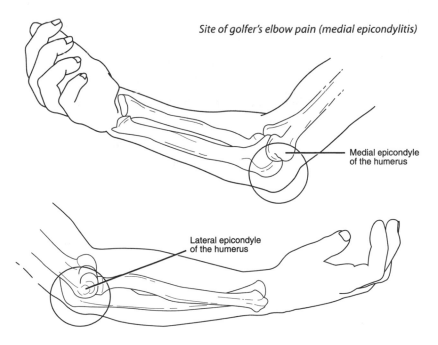

Site of golfer's elbow pain (medial epicondylitis)

Medial epicondyle of the humerus

Lateral epicondyle of the humerus

Site of tennis elbow pain (lateral epicondylitis)

cortisone injection. A course of ultrasound and transverse friction massage from a physical therapist may help the scar tissue forming during healing align with the healthy tendon fibers. In rare chronic cases, surgery may be required to clean out the accumulation of degenerated tissue.

Biceps Tendinitis and Rupture

With repetitive lifting or pulling, the biceps tendon can become inflamed, causing pain along the front crease of the elbow or closer to the shoulder. Ruptures of the tendon can occur, causing a noticeable cosmetic defect in the biceps as well as weakness, especially with the forearm rotated in the palm-upward position (supination).

As with other forms of tendinitis, rest from the offensive activity, use ice and NSAIDs, and gradually return to activity and strengthening once the pain subsides. A rupture requires medical attention and usually necessitates surgery.

Elbow Fracture

A break can occur in any of the three bones that meet at the elbow—the radius (in which case the fracture is known as a *radial head fracture*); the ulna (*olecranon fracture*); or the humerus (*supracondylar fracture*). Radial head fractures usually occur as a result of falling on an outstretched arm. Supracondylar fractures are rare in adults, and they occur as a result of a hard impact with the elbow bent, fracturing the area of the humerus just above the elbow. Olecranon fractures occur as a result of falling directly on the bony point of a bent elbow. Radial head and supracondylar fractures bring with them the potential for serious complications to the nerves and blood vessels that cross through the elbow joint supplying the forearms, wrists, hands, and fingers.

Elbow fractures should be considered medical emergencies because of the threat to the nerves and blood vessels that run through the joint and are close to the surface. The arm should be splinted or otherwise immobilized and, if possible, kept cool until medical assistance is available.

Olecranon Bursitis

Inflammation of the fluid-filled sac at the olecranon (bony tip of the elbow) is known as *olecranon bursitis*. It can be caused by a single, sharp blow to the tip, causing bleeding within the bursa (*hemobursitis*); or it can result from overuse if the edge of the elbow is subject to repeated stresses that cause the bursa to become inflamed. Pain and swelling are localized right at the pointy tip of the elbow. The swelling can be profuse, and you may feel radiating heat.

Ice and compression (using a foam donut centered around the bursa) can facilitate healing. If the condition interferes with range of motion, the bursa can be drained by a physician.

Ulnar Collateral Ligament Sprain

Partial or complete tearing of the ulnar collateral ligament (on the inside of the elbow joint) happens most commonly in throwers. Injury to this ligament may also affect the ulnar nerve, causing pain and tingling that radiates to the ring finger and little finger.

Rest and ice are helpful for the pain and inflammation. An orthopedist should be consulted.

Ulnar Nerve Impingement

The ulnar nerve runs in a groove along the medial (inner) side of your elbow. Excessive tension or inflammation in this area can cause the nerve to become irritated, causing a sharp, tingling pain (as if you had hit your funny bone) that radiates down toward the ring finger and little finger.

RICE and over-the-counter NSAIDs will generally lead to a complete resolution, though in severe chronic cases, surgery may be needed to relieve pressure on the nerve.

15

The Athletic Wrist and Hand

Thirty-seven muscles control the complex actions of your wrist and fingers. The wrist joint itself is formed by the lower (distal) ends of the two forearm bones, the radius and ulna, which articulate with several smaller bones (known as *carpals*). When you fall on your hand, you risk fracturing any of these bones, particularly the lower end of the radius and the *scaphoid*, one of the larger carpal bones that is adjacent to the end of the radius.

Structures of the Wrist and Hand

The hand's phenomenal dexterity owes a great deal to the multitude of small bones and joints contained within it.

Radiocarpal Joint

The *radiocarpal joint* is the main wrist joint, where the radius meets two smaller bones, known as carpals, on the thumb side of the wrist. One is called the scaphoid (the larger of the two carpal bones, and the one most important in terms of its position in the wrist) and the other is the *lunate*. There are six additional carpal bones that don't directly abut the radius.

Bones of the wrist and hand

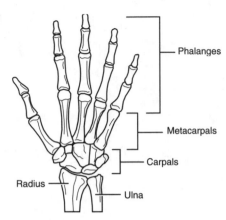

Trapeziometacarpal Joint

The *trapeziometacarpal joint* forms between one of the carpals, the *trapezoid*, and the base of your thumb. It's a unique type of joint called a *saddle joint*, which has a perfectly concave end on one bone that fits over a convex end of the adjacent bone, allowing for the thumb's circular range of motion. This circular motion, called *opposition*, is what enables you to perform a great deal of manual activity.

Metacarpals

The *metacarpals* are long, thin bones of your hand. These form joints with the carpal bones at the wrist and with the phalanges at the base of the fingers.

Phalanges

The *phalanges* are the smaller bones of your fingers, each of which has three joints above the palm.

Retinacula

Retinacula are thick, fibrous bands of connective tissue that wrap around the wrist, forming tunnels that protect the many tendons, blood vessels, and nerves of the hand and arm. The *flexor retinaculum* forms the carpal tunnel, which runs along the underside of your wrist. It encloses, in a tight area, several flexor tendons, as well as the median nerve.

Flexor and Extensor Digitori

The *flexor and extensor digitori* are muscles of the forearm that flex and extend each of the five fingers.

Ligaments

Numerous ligaments in the hand and wrist provide stability to the joints.

KJ TIP: Strengthening the Fingers

A variety of devices—ranging from a simple tennis ball to specially designed spring grips and gel-filled balls—are available to help increase finger strength. These products work by strengthening the muscles and tendons that flex and extend the wrists and fingers. They also provide a fast, easy way to warm up these areas before engaging in exercise.

Common Wrist and Hand Problems

Many wrist and hand injuries can be avoided with the use of protective gear.

Wrist Fractures

There are two common types of wrist fractures. The *distal radius fracture* is the most common sports-related fracture. It occurs just above the wrist, affecting the radius on the inner side. These fractures occur when you fall forward on your outstretched hand. Radius fractures cause pain and tenderness around the wrist. Symptoms may be minor enough that it feels like a sprain rather than a fracture.

A scaphoid fracture is a break in the scaphoid bone, a kidney-bean–shaped bone at the base of the thumb just above the wrist. You'll feel pain and swelling in the hollow on the side of the wrist just beneath the base of the thumb, an area referred to as the *snuffbox* because of the pocket it forms when your thumb is extended. Like fractures of the distal radius, this fracture also occurs commonly with falling on an outstretched hand. Because blood supply to this bone is poor, healing may be delayed, or may not occur at all without medical intervention.

Suspected wrist fractures need to be treated by a physician because of potential complications to the nerves, tendons, and blood vessels passing to the hand. Diagnosis can be difficult; small fractures may not show up on x-rays for one to two weeks.

Carpal Tunnel Syndrome

Carpal tunnel syndrome is the name for inflammation in the carpal tunnel causing compression of the median nerve, blood vessels, and tendons that pass across the bottom of the wrist and into the palm. The inflammation is usually triggered by overuse of the muscles and tendons crowded inside this narrow passageway. The pain can be dull and achy or tingling; sometimes it manifests itself as numbness or weakness in the thumb, index finger, or middle finger.

To treat, ice the area and refrain from exacerbating activities. Wear a wrist support brace, a device that allows the irritated structures of the wrist to rest. After recovery, key prevention involves strengthening the muscles by implementing resistive exercises for the wrist and fingers. If symptoms persist, you should see an orthopedist; severe cases of carpal tunnel syndrome might require surgery.

Ulnar Collateral Ligament Rupture or Sprain

A tear or rupture of the ulnar collateral ligament, the primary ligament connecting the metacarpal and phalangeal bones (*metacarpophalangeal joint*) of the thumb is often called *skier's thumb* or *gamekeeper's thumb*, because it occurs when the thumb is forced down and backward—for example, when falling on an outstretched arm while gripping a ski pole. Pain and swelling are present in the web space of the thumb. With severe ruptures, your thumb joint may feel loose and unstable as a result of damage to the ligament.

You should ice the injury and see a physician. Mild injuries can be treated with immobilization, followed by range-of-motion exercises. Complete ruptures, which are noticeable by the high degree of weakness and instability you'll feel in the thumb, may require surgery.

Flexor Tendon Strain or Rupture

A common injury among rock climbers, the primary finger tendon running though the forearm becomes stretched, inflamed, or torn through overuse.

Strains of the tendon should be treated with ice and rest from the aggravating activity. Ruptures are more serious and should have attention from an orthopedist specializing in treatment of the hand.

16

Strengthening and Flexibility Exercises

Flexibility and strength markedly decrease with age. Declining fluid content in the joints, erosion of cartilage, a decrease in the number of muscle fibers, and compression and loss of resilience to such soft tissue structures as ligaments and tendons contribute to loss of flexibility and strength—and are important factors in your increased susceptibility to injury.

You can enhance your performance and decrease your risk of injury by making stretching and strengthening exercises a daily part of your fitness routine. Unlike other fitness activities, stretching exercises require that you slow down, be patient, and relax as you "limber up" various parts of your body. Depending on your personal tastes, these exercises could be a welcome respite or a necessary annoyance. The keyword, however, is *necessary*. Even if you can only devote a few minutes a day, you should engage in a regular routine of flexibility and strengthening exercises.

Strengthening Exercises for the Foot, Ankle, and Lower Leg

The following exercises are designed to prevent and rehabilitate many injuries of the foot, ankle, and lower leg. Each exercise should be performed for one to three sets of 8 to 15 repetitions. The exercises should be done two to three times per week with at least one day of rest between sessions.

Towel Curl

Major muscles strengthened: Small intrinsic muscles of the foot

• Place a towel lengthwise on the floor in front of you, with the edge just beneath your toes.

• Begin pulling the towel under your foot while keeping the heel and forefoot stationary. Use only the toes.

• For added resistance, place a weight or heavy book on the end of the towel.

Slocums (Ankle Inversion)

Major muscles strengthened: Anterior and posterior tibialis

• Slip one end of rubber tubing around a table leg or chair leg adjacent to a chair you're sitting in.

• Loop the other end around the middle of the foot closest to the adjacent chair.

• Using the heel as a pivot, turn your ankle and foot inward, moving them as a single unit. Take care to keep your thigh and lower leg still.

• Hold and repeat.

Reverse Slocums (Ankle Eversion)

Major muscles strengthened: Peroneus longus and brevis

- Slip one end of rubber tubing around a table leg or chair leg.

- In a seated position, loop the other end around the middle of the foot located opposite the table or chair leg.

- Using the heel as a pivot, turn your ankle and foot outward. Take care to keep your thigh and lower leg still.

- Hold and repeat.

- Variation: Place the loop around both feet, and, with heels together and functioning as pivots, push balls of the feet apart. You can make this exercise more difficult by separating your feet, increasing the tension on the tubing.

Slocums and reverse slocums are excellent for strengthening major muscles controlling the foot and can be performed with a few cents' worth of surgical tubing or an old bicycle tire.

Eversion with Weights

Major muscles strengthened: Peroneus longus and brevis

- Lie on one side on an exercise bench or table with your upper foot dangling over the edge and a towel or foam wedge placed under your shin.

- Strap a cuff weight (three pounds should be sufficient) over the midsection of your foot.

- Relax your foot and allow it to point toward the floor.

- Raise your foot so that your little toe moves toward the ceiling without moving your lower leg. For best isolation of the peroneals, be careful not to move your foot up toward your knee, but rather toward the ceiling.

- Return to starting position and repeat.

- Roll over onto your other side and repeat with your other foot.

Inversion with Weights

Major muscles strengthened: Anterior tibialis, posterior tibialis

- Same as Eversion with Weights, except the foot you will be exercising is the lower one, raising your big toe toward the ceiling.

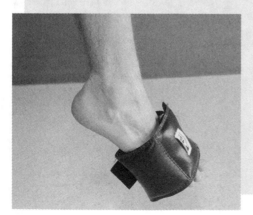

You can strengthen your foot and ankle with a simple weight band. Among the exercises you can perform are dorsiflexion (shown) and eversion and inversion.

Isometric Dorsiflexion

Major muscles strengthened: Anterior tibialis

- With your heel on the ground in a fixed position, lift the forefoot off the ground.

- Place the heel of your other foot flat above the top of your exercising foot.

- While pressing down with the top foot, dorsiflex the lower foot to maximum contraction. Hold for a count of 10. Repeat 10 times.

Isometric Plantarflexion

Major muscles strengthened: Gastrocnemius, soleus, posterior tibialis

- Sit on the floor with your leg outstretched and the bottom surface of your foot against a wall.

- Press the ball of your foot into the wall.

- Hold and repeat.

Toe Raises (Calf Raises)

Major muscles strengthened: Gastrocnemius, soleus, posterior tibialis

- Stand on a step, the balls of your feet near the edge.

- Take two counts to slowly raise yourself up on your toes.

- Take four counts to slowly lower yourself back to the starting position.

- Variations: Perform the exercise while squeezing a tennis ball between your heels to emphasize the peroneal muscles. To emphasize the eccentric function of the calf muscles, use both legs to raise yourself up, but lower yourself down with just one leg.

Toe raises can be done with weights, as shown here, or by simply standing on the edge of a step. Variations include performing the movement with toes in or toes out, or squeezing a tennis ball between the heels as you perform the movement.

Heel Raises

Major muscles strengthened: Tibialis anterior

- Beginning with your foot flat on the ground, lift the heel about an inch off the ground.

- Balance and hold.

- Lower and repeat.

Ankle Proprioception Exercises

While these exercises target all the muscles of the lower leg, ankle, and foot, their main function is to train the proprioceptors of the ankle joint. Proprioceptors function to give your brain information about where your body is in space. They also act as your early warning mechanism for impending injury. The following activities can help you improve your proprioception:

- Balance while standing on one foot with your knee slightly bent.

- While standing balanced on one foot with your knee slightly bent, move your opposite leg in random directions.

- Play catch while balancing on one foot with a slight bend in your knee.

- Balance on a wobble board or balance platform (a circular platform with a ball on the bottom).

Flexibility Exercises for the Foot, Ankle, and Lower Leg

Warm up first. Hold each stretch for 10 to 30 seconds. Do not bounce. If you have orthotics, you should perform the calf stretches with your orthotics and shoes on so that your arch does not collapse and you can get the maximum benefit from the stretch.

Slantboard Stretch

- Use a slantboard with an approximately 35-degree incline—you can lean one edge of a board against a stack of books.

- Place your foot on the board, toes higher than heels.

- Hold, then repeat with the other foot.

Wall Stretch

- Stand two to four feet away from a wall, with one foot in front of the other.

- Lean into the wall in a semi-lunge position, bending the front leg and keeping the back leg straight.

- Keeping both feet flat on the ground, push your body weight into the rear leg.

- Press your upper body closer to the wall to intensify the stretch. Make sure the heel stays down.

- Switch legs and repeat.

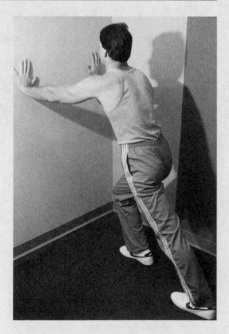

Wall stretch

Bent-Knee Wall Stretch

- Stand slightly closer to the wall than in the Wall Stretch, with one foot in front of the other.

- Lean into the wall in a semilunge position, bending the rear leg as well as the forward leg.

- Keeping both feet flat on the ground, push your body weight into the rear leg.

- You should feel this stretch deep and low in the calf. If you feel it in the front of your ankle instead, move your feet closer to the wall.

- Switch legs and repeat.

Pointed Toe Stretch

- Kneel on the floor, back straight, hands at your side for balance.

- Point your toes so that your body weight rests on your forefoot.

- Bring your body weight down over your feet to a point that's comfortable.

- You should not perform this stretch if you have a history of knee problems.

Plantar Fascia Stretch

- Reach down and grasp the ball of your foot.

- Pull up on the foot to the point of maximum extension.

- Hold.

- Repeat with other foot. This stretch can be done in a sitting or standing position.

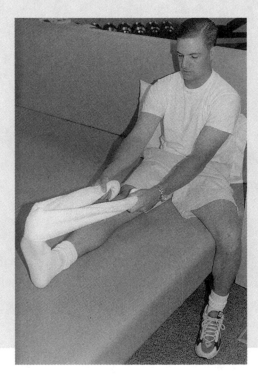

The plantar fascia stretch can be done in a sitting or standing position.

Strengthening Exercises for the Hip and Thigh

Follow the guidelines for strengthening set forth in the prior sections. Each exercise should be performed for one to three sets of 8 to 15 repetitions. The exercises should be done two to three times per week with at least one day of rest between sessions.

Hip Extension

Major muscles strengthened: Gluteus maximus, hamstrings, back extensors

- This can be done either using a machine at the gym (multihip machine or cable–pulley system) or with a cuff weight or stretchy band around your ankle.

- Keep your trunk erect as you extend your thigh backward. Pause at the end of the motion, and then slowly return to the starting position.

- Be sure to tighten your abdominal muscles so that you don't hyperextend your back.

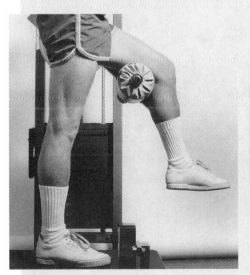 

A multihip machine, found in many health clubs, can be used to perform a variety of exercises, including the hip extension (shown above). Keep your trunk erect and your abdominals tight as you perform the motion.

Hip Abduction

Major muscles strengthened: Gluteus medius, tensor fascia lata

- This can be done using a machine at the gym (multihip or abduction/adduction machine) or using a cuff weight or stretchy band around your ankle.

- As you keep your trunk upright and your pelvis level, lift your leg out to the side, away from your centerline. Pause at the end of the motion, and then slowly return to the starting position.

- The motion will be relatively small. Do not go to the point where your trunk begins to tip to the side.

Hip Adduction

Major muscles strengthened: Adductor muscle group of the inner thigh

This exercise is done in the same manner and with the same equipment as hip abduction, but the resistance will be against the muscles that you use to pull your leg in toward your midline.

Hip abduction and hip adduction using the multihip machine. An ankle weight or stretchy bands can be used to perform the exercises as well.

Squat

Major muscles strengthened: Gluteus maximus, quadriceps, hamstrings

- The squat is done in a standing position, with your feet hip-width apart. You can use a squat machine, a free-weight barbell on your shoulders, or even just your body weight, as described in the Chair Squat exercise (page 193).

- In a slow, controlled manner, bend your knees, keeping them aligned over your toes. You should not bend them any more than 90 degrees. In fact, the farther you bend, the more compressive force is applied to your knee joint. Since most activity requires only 30 to 60 degrees of knee flexion, a partial squat is very effective in strengthening the quads in the functional range while avoiding increased compression to the joint. Pause at the bottom, and then return to the starting position.

It's not important to go into a deep knee bend when performing squats, and it may in fact lead to injury. Instead, perform a partial squat, pausing several degrees before your thighs become parallel with the floor.

KJ TIP: Proper Movement

It's important to exercise the components responsible for eccentric motions using the calf muscles, hamstrings, and quadriceps. To effectively do so, use weight machines and select a weight that you can lift with both legs. At maximum contraction, use only one leg to return the weight to the starting position, and do so in a slow, controlled manner.

Chair Squat

Major muscles strengthened: Gluteus maximus, quadriceps, hamstrings

- Put one chair behind you, and rest your hands on the back of a second one in front of you.

- Stand erect, your feet slightly wider than shoulder width, toes pointed slightly out.

- Come down slowly until your buttocks barely touch the seat.

- Keep your gaze slightly up, your back as straight and perpendicular as possible.

- Pause for a count of five while isometrically contracting the muscles in the legs and buttocks.

- Slowly return to the starting position. The motion of rising should come from both the heels and toes of your foot, which remain firmly planted throughout the motion.

- You can increase the exercise intensity by holding the squat position for a longer period of time during each rep and by coming down slowly. You'll feel the tension along the entire front of your thigh.

Leg Press

Major muscles strengthened: Gluteus maximus, quadriceps, hamstrings

- This exercise is done on a leg press machine.

- Adjust the platform so that when you are on the machine, your knees are bent no more than 90 degrees in the starting position.

- Place your feet on the platform at shoulder width.

- Slowly extend the knee, being careful not to lock it out.

KJ CLOSEUP: Avoiding Knee Injuries

- Hyaline cartilage—the substance that lines the surfaces of the bones where one bone comes in contact with another bone to form a joint—can be coaxed into expanding for greater shock absorption with a few moments of warm-up exercise. Before any activity that involves the knee, warm up first with mild cardiovascular exercise and then with slow partial (less than one-third of a full squat) knee bends.

- If you have had a serious knee injury, avoid contact sports and distance running. Both activities have a high risk of knee injury. Patellofemoral pain syndrome—irritation of the articular cartilage behind the kneecap—is highest among distance runners (which is why it's often dubbed *runner's knee*). If you're a committed runner experiencing knee pain, consider reducing your mileage and adding swimming and cycling to your aerobic mix.

- Be careful on the slopes. Ski season brings in a shockingly high number of injuries, most commonly tears of the menisci and the medial collateral and anterior cruciate ligaments. There are three steps you can take to minimize your risk of skiing-related knee injuries:

  * For six weeks before the season, strengthen the quadriceps, hamstrings, and calf muscles.

  * Make sure your boots fit well and that the quick releases work properly.

  * Start late, and quit early. Most injuries occur early in the day or late in the day. Decline the "just-one-more-run" syndrome.

Leg Extension

Major muscles strengthened: Quadriceps

- Use a leg extension machine or ankle weights.

- Begin with extremely light weight (or no weight).

- Seated, with leg bent at no more than a 90-degree angle, slowly extend your leg straight out while contracting the muscles of the quadriceps against resistance.

- Extend to the point where your knee is almost straight. (Straightening it completely may cause irritation of your patellofemoral joint.)

- Slowly return to the starting position.

- If you feel any pain during the movement, perform the exercise only up to that point, and then return to starting position.

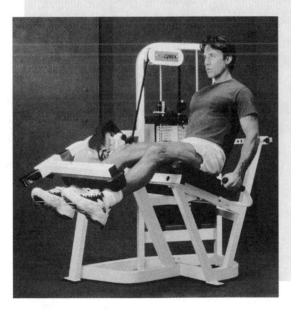

Leg extension (photo courtesy of Cybex Corp.)

Isometric Quadriceps Exercise

Major muscles strengthened: Quadriceps

- Perform this exercise either seated or standing parallel to a wall.

- Extend your leg fully, and squeeze your quadriceps to maximal contraction. Hold for a count of 10.

- As you're extending your leg, push outward toward your foot, "lengthening" the leg as if you were trying to touch the opposite wall with the sole of your foot.

Hamstring Curl

Major muscles strengthened: Hamstrings

- Use extremely light weight or no weight for the first few sessions.

- This exercise can be done using a leg curl machine or lying on your stomach and using a cuff weight around your ankle. (If using a leg curl machine, adjust the pad so that it rests above the Achilles tendon.)

- Raise the weight slowly. Pause, and then lower the weight slowly in a controlled manner. The eccentric contraction is important in exercising the hamstrings.

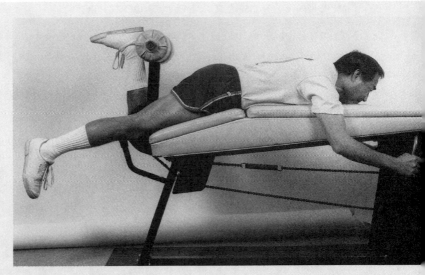

When doing the hamstring curl, it's important to emphasize the eccentric motion, so use a weight that requires both legs to lift, but then use only one leg to slowly lower the weight to the starting position.

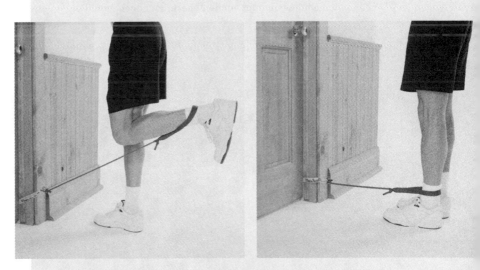

Hamstring curls can also be performed in a standing position, using a stretchy band (photos courtesy of Hygenic Corp.).

Flexibility Exercises for the Hip and Thigh

Follow the guidelines set forth in previous sections for stretching. Warm up first. Hold each stretch for 10 to 30 seconds. Do not bounce during a stretch.

Hamstring Stretch

- Seated on a workout bench, place one foot on the floor, and extend the other leg in front of you. If you do not have a workout bench available to you, sit on the ground with the leg you are stretching extended in front of you and the other leg bent at the knee. You can also kneel on one knee, with the leg you are stretching extended in front of you, as long as you do not have any problems with the knee you are kneeling on.

- Gently lean forward over your outstretched leg. The stretch should come from your hips, not your back. Your back should be straight and not curved during the stretch. If you do it properly, you will feel the stretch in the hips, lower back, gluteus, and the back of the upper legs.

The hamstring stretch should be done with one leg at a time.

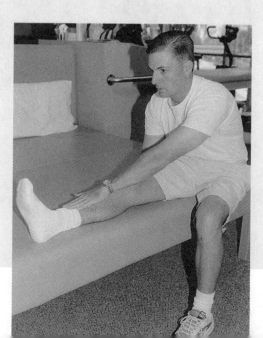

Standing Quadriceps Stretch

- Place your hand on a chair or wall for balance.

- Bring your leg up behind you and grasp the top of your foot or your ankle.

- Pull the leg in gently toward your buttocks. Be sure to keep your trunk erect. Do not lean forward.

- Alternate stretch position: Rest the top of your foot behind you against a wall or low table top and gently press your body back for a full, even stretch of the quadriceps.

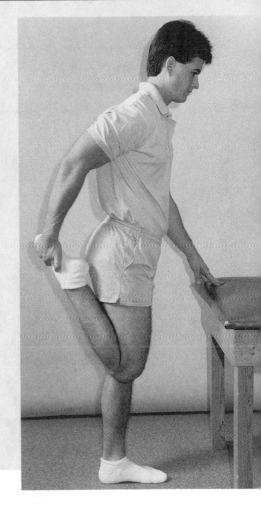

The standing quadriceps stretch

Iliotibial Band Stretch

- Lie on your back.

- Raise the leg you are going to stretch upward and drop it across your body until your foot touches the floor. Let the hip on that side come up off the floor.

- You may feel this stretch anywhere along the ITB, from the hip down to the knee.

- Alternate stretch position: In a standing position, cross the leg you are going to stretch behind the other leg. Bend forward, and turn toward the rear foot.

(Note: This stretch position is not recommended if you have a history of back pain.)

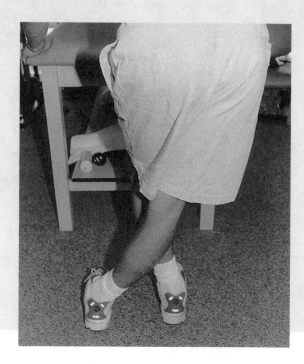

Alternate position for iliotibial band stretch

Strengthening Exercises for the Back and Abdomen

During all exercises for your trunk, it is important to hold your spine in proper posture—the neutral spine position, where the normal curves that belong in your spine are maintained. Additionally, you should strengthen the powerful muscles of the hips and legs so that you can use them for lifting heavy objects instead of using your back.

Follow the guidelines for strengthening exercises. Perform one to three sets of 8 to 15 repetitions. In addition to the exercises presented here, you can also try the Hip Extension, which appears on page 189. Do the exercises two to three times per week, with at least one day of rest between exercise sessions.

Active Back Hyperextension

- Lie on your stomach with one or two pillows under your stomach.
- Clasp your hands and rest them above your buttocks, behind your head, or at your sides.
- Slowly lift your head and trunk. Do not extend beyond the position shown in the photo.
- Pause, and then slowly return to the starting position.

Active back hyperextension performed with hands behind head

KJ CLOSEUP: The Abdominal Muscles—
Important Function, Simple Exercise

In every sport and movement, the midsection of the body is the primary channel for transferring force and impact between the upper and lower extremities. So it's difficult to imagine any athletic activity being performed efficiently with weak abdominals. At the same time, most people become overwhelmed by the conflicting regimens of abdominal exercises touted in various magazines. A few pointers:

- *Losing fat:* Abdominal fat and a strong abdomen are not mutually exclusive. To lose abdominal fat, you need to decrease your total body fat. This is done by increasing the number of calories burned and decreasing the number of calories ingested. In other words, eat less and do more aerobic exercise. The fact that fat, in many men, accumulates around the abdomen doesn't mean it can be eliminated merely through abdominal exercises, or *spot reduction*, as it's sometimes called. Spot reduction doesn't work.

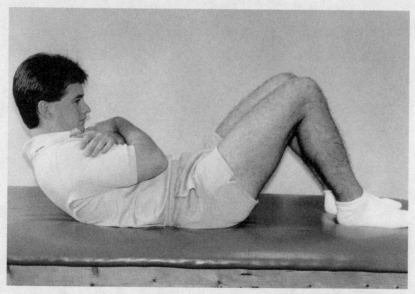

Studies show that the partial sit-up curl can hit all facets of the abdominal muscles.

- *Building abdominal strength:* While you can't target the abs for weight loss, you can target them for strength. By building the muscle, you're also increasing your body's ability to burn calories, so you are indirectly triggering an overall reduction in body fat.

- *Four muscles, one exercise:* The abdominals include four muscle groups: the internal and external obliques, which rotate your torso and allow you to bend from side to side; and the transverse and rectus abdominis muscles, which flex your trunk forward over your lower body. While there are a variety of different abdominal exercises you can perform—you've probably seen countless forms of sit-ups being done in the gym, to say nothing of the ubiquitous abdominal "roller" devices—studies have shown that just one will work all these different muscles, and it's a safe way to do it. It's the partial sit-up curl, and it works like this: Lie flat on your back, knees bent at a 45-degree angle. Cross your arms over your chest, tuck your chin toward your chest, and lift your torso until your shoulder blades clear the ground, keeping the muscles contracted throughout the motion. Pause at the top and come back down slowly. Repeat for four sets of 8 to 12 repetitions. When the motion becomes too easy, you can place a weight under your crossed arms to add resistance.

Flexibility Exercises for the Back

Follow the guidelines set forth in previous sections for stretching. Hold each stretch for 10 to 30 seconds. Do not bounce.

Trunk Rotation

- Lie on your side on the floor with your knees and hips flexed at 90 degrees.

- Place your lower hand on top of your knees.

- Leading with your upper arm, which is straight and extended, begin rotating from your shoulders, through your trunk and hips, trying to get your upper shoulder blade as close to the ground as is comfortably possible.

- At the point of maximum stretch, hold. Then come back slowly to the original position.

- Repeat on the opposite side.

This is the point of maximum stretch for trunk rotation. Your starting position is on your side, in a semifetal position.

Cat Stretch

- Kneel on all fours, elbow straight.
- Arch your back slowly upward, like a cat.
- Relax your head, letting it hang between your shoulders.
- The stretch is in the center of your spine—it should feel as if an invisible string is pulling it toward the ceiling.
- Slowly let your back sink until it's arching downward.
- Push your buttocks high and back, bring your head up, and look toward the ceiling.
- Repeat 10 times.

Cat-Prayer Stretch

- Start out as in the Cat Stretch (above).
- After arching your back, begin pushing back from your shoulders, bringing your buttocks down toward your heels.
- Stretch as far back as possible until you are sitting on your heels.
- Hold and repeat.

The cat stretch exercises help improve the strength and flexibility of the spine and back. To go into the cat–prayer position, push back until the buttocks touch the heels.

Knee to Chest

- Lie on your back with your knees bent, feet flat on the floor.
- Bring one knee up toward your chest.
- Grasp behind your thigh with both hands, and pull the leg in slowly toward your chest.
- Hold, then return to starting position and repeat with opposite leg.

Standing Extension

- Stand with your feet shoulder-width apart, knees very slightly bent.
- Place your hands against the ridge of your lower back, just over the top of your buttocks.
- Your posture should be tall and straight.
- Bend gently backward as far as is comfortable while supporting your lower back with your hands. You should feel as if you are pushing your hips forward.
- Hold, then return slowly to the starting position and repeat.

Thoracic Extension

- Sit tall in a chair.
- Place your clasped hands behind your neck.
- Lean back over the edge of the chair's back.
- Let gravity pull your head downward to a comfortable stretch.
- Hold, then slowly return to the starting position and repeat.

Seated Thoracic Flexion

- Sit in a chair with your back straight, head erect, and feet flat on the floor and slightly farther than shoulder-width apart.

- With your hands clasped in front of you, bend forward from the waist, gradually increasing the curve of your back until your torso reaches the point of maximum stretch between your legs.

- You should feel the stretch along your back.

- Hold, then slowly return to the starting position.

Floor Thoracic Flexion

- Sit on the floor with your knees bent and feet flat on the floor.

- Clasp your hands around your knees.

- Slowly tuck your chin in toward your chest.

- Relax and lean back, curving the spine for a maximum stretch.

- Hold, then return to the starting position and repeat.

Trunk Twist

- Sit on the floor with your legs extended in front of you.

- Bend your right knee and place your right foot against the outer side of your left knee.

- Put your right hand on the floor behind you for support.

- Place your bent left elbow against the outer part of your right knee, just above the thigh.

- Using your right hand and left elbow to aid in the pivot, twist from the lower back up through the mid-spine, and hold at the maximum stretch.

- Hold, then repeat on the opposite side.

The trunk twist stretches the structures of the back and hip.

Strengthening Exercises for the Shoulder

Follow the guidelines for strengthening set forth in the prior sections. Each exercise should be performed for one to three sets of 8 to 15 repetitions. The exercises should be done two to three times per week, with at least one day of rest between sessions.

Shoulder Flexion

Major muscle strengthened: Anterior deltoid

- Stand or sit with your arm at your side, holding a weight with your palm toward your thigh.
- Keeping your elbow straight, raise your arm in front of you, leading with the thumb.
- Continue slowly until your arm is overhead.
- Return slowly to the starting position and repeat.

Shoulder Abduction

Major muscles strengthened: Middle deltoid, supraspinatus

- Stand with your arms at your sides, loosely clutching dumbbells.
- Lift your arms outward to shoulder height, keeping your elbows straight.
- Lower arms slowly to starting position and repeat.
- To decrease the risk of injury, raise the dumbbells until the arms are parallel to the floor but no higher. If you experience pain when lifting your arms to 90 degrees, stop before you get to that point.

Rotator Cuff Elevation

Major muscle strengthened: Supraspinatus

- Stand with your arms at your sides, holding light weights in your hands.

- Keeping your elbows straight, turn your arms in so that your thumbs are pointing downward (as if you were emptying out a beverage can).

- Bring your arms forward to an angle slightly in front your body.

- Raise your arms 80 degrees (just below parallel with the ground), keeping your elbows extended and your thumbs pointed downward toward the floor.

- Slowly lower your arms to the starting position and repeat.

- Variation: If you are not experiencing any shoulder pain, you can try a more advanced version of this exercise. Begin the exercise as outlined. When you get to 80 degrees of elevation, flip your hands so that your thumb points up. Continue to raise your arms until they are overhead. When you lower your arm back down, flip your hands so that your thumb points down again as you pass through 80 degrees.

Rotator cuff elevation should be performed slowly, and the movement should end just before your arms become parallel with the ground.

Shoulder Shrug

Major muscles strengthened: Upper trapezius and levator scapulae

- Stand with your arms at your side, weights lightly grasped in your hands, feet shoulder-width apart.
- With the elbows slightly flexed, shrug your shoulders, lifting them up and back toward your ears.
- Return to the starting position and repeat.

Military Press

Major muscles strengthened: Deltoids

- Sit with the weights held at about shoulder height.
- Press your arms straight overhead with the palms facing in. Take care not to arch your back excessively.
- Return slowly to the starting position.

Horizontal Shoulder Abduction

Major muscles strengthened: Posterior deltoid, rhomboids, middle trapezius

- Stand next to a table or bench, leaning forward from the hips, with your arm perpendicular to the floor. Use your other arm to support your body weight on the table or bench.
- Keeping your elbow straight, lift your arm up to the side until it's parallel to the floor—but don't bring it any higher than the point at which it's level with your shoulder.
- Return slowly to the starting position and repeat.

Rowing

Major muscles strengthened: Rhomboids, middle trapezius, latissimus dorsi

- Stand next to a table or bench.
- Lean forward from the hips, using the arm closest to the bench for support of your body weight. Allow the other arm, which is holding the weight, to dangle to the floor.
- Pull backward, bending your elbow, in a rowing motion.
- Slowly return to the starting position and repeat.

Shoulder Extension

Major muscles strengthened: Latissimus dorsi, lower trapezius

- Stand next to a table or bench.
- Lean forward from the hips, using the arm closest to the bench for support of your body weight. Allow the other arm, which is loosely clasping a weight, to hang perpendicular to the floor.
- Bring the arm backward, keeping your elbow straight, until it's parallel to your trunk.
- Return the weight slowly to the starting position and repeat the motion.

External Rotation

Major muscles strengthened: Infraspinatus, teres minor

- On a table, bench, or the floor, lie on your side.
- Place a towel roll between the elbow of the arm on the upper side and your trunk.

- Holding a weight in the hand opposite the side you're lying on, keep the elbow against the towel roll, bent at 90 degrees.

- Rotate your arm, lifting your hand toward the ceiling, keeping your elbow against the towel.

- Return slowly to the starting position and repeat.

External rotation can be performed lying on your side with a light dumbbell. Moving your forearm only, raise the weight toward the ceiling.

- Variation: This exercise can also be done in a standing position. Pull against surgical tubing that is attached to a doorknob or other stationary object. The elbow should be kept at 90 degrees, with a space between the elbow and the trunk, as the arm is rotated outward.

External rotation, in standing position, with surgical tubing

Internal Rotation

Major muscles strengthened: Subscapularis, pectoralis major

- Lie on your side; a pillow or soft pad placed under the side of your chest, beneath the armpit, will make this exercise more comfortable.

- Hold a weight in the hand on the same side you're lying on.

- Your elbow should be bent to 90 degrees and resting slightly in front of your trunk.

- Slowly lift your forearm toward your chest, keeping the elbow angle constant. The only movement should come from your shoulder.

- Return slowly to the starting position. Repeat on the other side.

- Variation: This exercise can also be done in a standing position by pulling against surgical tubing that is attached to a doorknob or other stationary object. The elbow should be kept at 90 degrees as the arm is rotated inward.

Internal rotation, an important rotator cuff exercise, can also be performed standing, as shown above (photos courtesy of Cybex Corp.).

Horizontal Adduction

Major muscle strengthened: Pectoralis major

- Lie on your back on a workout bench, weights in your hands.

- Hold your arms out to the side with the elbows straight and the palms facing the ceiling.

- Raise the weights toward each other and the ceiling.

- Lower slowly to the horizontal position, taking care not to let your arms go beyond the plane of your body. Repeat.

KJ CLOSEUP: Push-ups and Chin-ups

These two simple exercises can effectively exercise many of the muscles of the upper body. However, correct technique is essential to avoid injury. When performing a push-up, refrain from using push-up handles and from lowering your body below shoulder level; while this provides an extra stretch to the pectoral muscles, it causes a slight subluxation of the humerus in the glenoid fossa, which can stretch and damage the joint capsule and ligaments of the shoulder. In contrast, arching the area between the shoulder blades at the upper part of the push-up (a movement known as a *push-up plus*) has the beneficial effect of strengthening the scapular muscles.

Chin-up exercises strengthen the muscles in back of the shoulder, including the trapezius and the latissimus dorsi, as well as the biceps muscles of the arms. They should be done slowly and carefully—make sure not to twist or kick while pulling your body up, because that will predispose you to injury. It's better to use proper form for fewer repetitions than to use poor form for more repetitions. To avoid excessive traction on the shoulder at the bottom end of the motion, which could stretch the shoulder capsule, put a stool under your feet at a height that allows for a slight bend in the elbows while grasping the bar.

Push-up with a Plus

Major muscles strengthened: Pectoralis major, triceps, serratus anterior

- Lie on the floor on your stomach. Place your hands at shoulder level, with arms bent and elbows hugged to the side.

- Keeping your back and legs straight, straighten your arms and lift your whole body from your toes.

- At the top of the motion, give an extra push, rounding the area between your shoulder blades.

- Lower slowly, being careful not to bend your elbows greater than 90 degrees. Repeat.

- Variation: If the standard push-up is too difficult, it can be modified so that the starting position is on your hands and knees.

If done with an extra push at the end of the motion, the push-up will strengthen the scapular muscles in addition to the pectoralis and triceps muscles.

Chin-up

Major muscles strengthened: Latissimus dorsi, biceps, lower trapezius, rhomboids

- Stand facing the chin-up station. Grasp the bar with palms facing you.
- Pull your body up to the bar until your chin is level with your hands.
- Lower yourself slowly to the starting position.

Flexibility Exercises for the Shoulder

Follow the guidelines set forth in previous sections for stretching. Warm up first. Hold each stretch for 10 to 30 seconds. Do not bounce into a stretch.

Shoulder Pendulums

An excellent warm-up exercise to precede shoulder flexibility and strengthening exercises.

- Stand next to a table or bench.
- Bend your trunk at the waist, and use the arm closest to the bench to support your body weight.
- Let the opposite arm hang loosely in front of you.
- Rotate the arm in a clockwise direction, drawing imaginary circles on the ground below, 30 times.
- Rotate the arm counterclockwise 30 times.
- Move the arm from side to side.
- Move the arm forward and backward.

Shoulder pendulums can be done as a warm-up before shoulder flexibility and strengthening exercises.

Shoulderblade Spread

- In a standing position, reach around in a hugging motion and hold your shoulder blades.

- Drop your chin down and lean slightly forward. Hold. Repeat.

Rhomboid Stretch

- Face an open door or a pole.

- With your feet firmly planted at the base of the pole or door, place your hands on the doorknobs or on the pole and lower your body into a seated position.

- Keep your arms straight and feel the stretch between your shoulder blades. Hold. Repeat.

Superior Rotator Cuff and Capsule Stretch

- With a towel roll in your armpit, place your forearm squarely against the ridge of your lower back.

- Reach around with the opposite hand, grab your wrist, and pull straight across your back. Hold.

- Repeat on the opposite side.

Posterior Rotator Cuff and Capsule Stretch

- Lift your arm to shoulder height and bring it across your body, placing it just beneath your chin.

- With the opposite hand, grab your arm at the elbow and pull inward across your chest. Hold.

- Repeat on the opposite side. If you experience pain in your shoulder during this stretch, try lowering your arm to below the horizontal plane.

Posterior rotator cuff and capsule stretch

Inferior Rotator Cuff and Capsule Stretch

- Lift your arm above your head, elbow bent back behind you.

- Use your other hand to pull the elbow slightly behind your head. Hold.

- Repeat on the opposite side.

Inferior rotator cuff and capsule stretch

Wall Climb

- Stand facing a wall, with your feet approximately six inches away from the wall.

- Place your hand flat against the wall at shoulder height.

- Walk your fingers up the wall to full flexion, and then back down again.

- Repeat on other side.

- This exercise can also be done with your side to the wall.

Strengthening Exercises for the Wrist, Forearm, and Elbow

Follow the guidelines for strengthening set forth in the prior sections. Each exercise should be performed for one to three sets of 8 to 15 repetitions. The exercises should be done two to three times per week, with at least one day of rest between sessions.

Biceps Curl

Major muscles strengthened: Biceps

- Stand grasping a weight in each hand.

- Bend your elbow in a controlled manner. Do not use momentum to lift the weight.

- Lower the weight slowly back to the starting position.

Triceps Extension

Major muscle strengthened: Triceps

- Lie on your back.

- With a weight in your hand, stretch your arm up toward the ceiling. Your elbow should be straight.

- Keeping your upper arm stationary, bend your elbow slowly, lowering the weight.

- Raise the weight back up to the starting position.

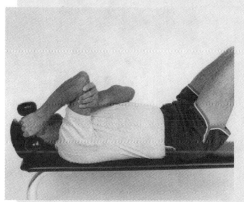

Triceps extension

Wrist Curl (Wrist Flexion)

Major muscles strengthened: Wrist flexors

- While seated, place your forearm either on your lap or on a table in front of you, palm facing up.

- Grasp a dumbbell or weight bar, palm up.

- Slowly lower your hand, allowing your wrist to extend fully.

- Moving only your wrist, curl the weight upward as high as you can, and hold before slowly lowering it again.

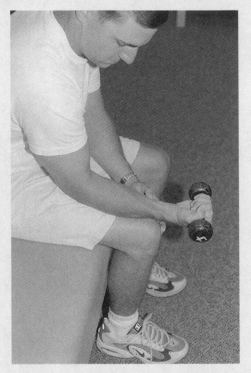

Wrist curl

Reverse Wrist Curl (Wrist Extension)

Major muscles strengthened: Wrist extensors

- Same as the Wrist Curl (Wrist Flexion), except the palm faces downward.

Wrist Pronation/Supination

Major muscles strengthened: Biceps, pronator teres, supinator

- Use a bar, 10 to 12 inches long, weighted on one end. (This is easily purchased in any sporting goods store, and is well worth it, particularly if you play racket sports.)

- With the bar in your hand, rest your forearm on your thigh or on a table in front of you with the hand hanging off the edge, and stabilize its position by placing the opposite hand on the center of your forearm.

- Rotate your forearm from a palm-up to a palm-down position, in smooth, even arcs.

- Repeat for the other arm. Build up to 3 sets of 12 reps.

Radial Deviation

Major muscles strengthened: Wrist flexors and extensors on the radial (thumb) side of the forearm

- Use a bar weighted on one end.

- Stand with your arm at your side and your elbow straight.

- Hold the end of the bar in your hand with the weight facing forward.

- Using only your wrist, tilt the bar up, leading with your thumb.

- Slowly lower to the starting position.

- Repeat on the opposite side.

Ulnar Deviation

Major muscles strengthened: Wrist flexors and extensors on the ulnar (little finger) side of the forearm

- Use a bar weighted on one end.
- Stand with your arm at your side and your elbow straight.
- Hold the end of the bar in your hand with the weight plate facing backward.
- Using only your wrist, tilt the weight upward behind you, slowly and evenly.
- Slowly lower to the starting position.
- Repeat on the opposite side.

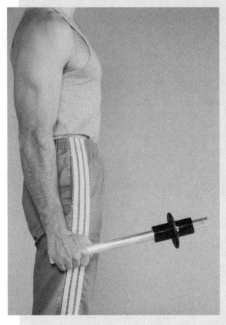 

Radial deviation and ulnar deviation are excellent fore-arm strengtheners and are performed with a bar weighted on only one end.

Flexibility Exercises for the Wrist, Forearm, and Elbow

Follow the guidelines set forth in previous sections for stretching. Warm up first. Hold each stretch for 10 to 30 seconds. Do not bounce into a stretch.

Wrist Flexor Stretch

- In a seated or standing position, with your elbow straight, extend your wrist back so that your palm faces away from your body and your fingers point downward.

- With the free hand, gently pull your fingers in toward your body to the point of maximum stretch. You'll feel the stretch up and down the bottom of your wrist and forearm.

- Hold and repeat. Then do it on the opposite side.

- Variation: You can also do this stretch by standing and placing your palm flat on a table or bench with your fingers pointing toward your body.

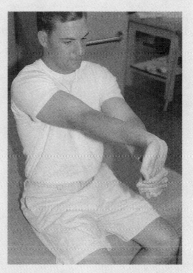

The wrist flexor stretch will stretch the structures on the palm side of your forearm.

Wrist Extensor Stretch

- Stand with your arm at your side, elbow straight.

- Flex your wrist so that the back of your hand faces the floor.

- Use your hand to increase the amount of flexion in your wrist by pulling the hand up slightly.

- Hold at the point of maximum stretch. You'll feel the stretch along the top of your wrist and forearm. Repeat.

- Repeat on the opposite side.

The Kerlan-Jobe Athlete's Resource Guide

PART 3

17

Common Sense Tips
for the Athlete

We've compiled this section to address a variety of practical factors that can improve your ability to pursue the physical activities you enjoy. These tips have been successfully used by elite athletes around the world.

Periodization: A Schedule for Fitness

Periodization, developed for Olympic athletes in the 1960s, provides a sensible system for fitness and sports training in which you cycle your body through varying levels of intensity throughout the year. As a result, you avoid overtraining and injury. In addition, by looking at each year as four individual units, you can stay fresh by altering your activities and interests while remaining fit.

Periodization divides your fitness program into blocks of time and training elements. There are two types of time blocks.

Macrocycles

Macrocycles are the largest unit of time. For elite athletes, the macrocycle is usually one or two years long; for recreational athletes, however, it can be a manageable three months. You should define a specific goal for your macrocycle. For example, if you plan on skiing in the winter, you can state your objective as follows: *To get in peak condition for skiing, thus avoiding the possibility of soreness and injury that is associated with many ski trips.* If you decide to play a sport you've never attempted before—soccer, for example—you can state your objective as follows: *To develop basic skills, strength, and endurance for playing soccer.*

Mesocycle

A month-long unit of time in your exercise schedule is a *mesocycle.* Each month focuses on a different phase.

- *First mesocycle:* This is the phase in which you prepare your body for increasing demands. Your focus will be on general conditioning, doing exercises at high volume and low intensity—in other words, light weights with lots of repetitions, and light aerobic exercises.
- *Second mesocycle:* In this phase, identify and focus on exercises specific to your sport. For skiing, you would work on strength and endurance exercises for the legs and trunk, and spend ample time on technique. You can spend two or three days a week on the conditioning exercises, and two days a week on technique. (Consult an off-season ski coach. In addition, many cities now have health clubs with ski trainers that have hydraulically controlled platforms that simulate a ski slope.)

  At the same time, spend one session per week continuing your general conditioning exercises. If your health club has a simulated ski machine, make use of it. In this phase, you can lower the volume of your exercises while increasing the intensity (heavier weights with fewer repetitions, more intense aerobic exercise).
- *Third mesocycle:* For the first two weeks of this third cycle, continue to increase the intensity of your sport-specific and general conditioning exercises, and increase your focus on proper form and technique. For the second two weeks, reduce your conditioning exercises and focus exclusively on proper form and technique. This taper allows your body to recover and incorporate the gains you've made.

> **KJ FACT: The Taper**
> Studies have shown that when athletes *taper,* or dramatically reduce their volume of training one to three weeks before a major event, their performance during the event improves, a sign that a well-conditioned body thrives on rest and recovery.

After completing a macrocycle, allow your body time to transition. Ease off, and your body will continue to become stronger as it repairs itself. If you continue to push yourself, however, you'll begin to experience declines in performance and strength. Adaptation will become maladaptation. So enjoy this period of time.

During this transition, you can begin to think about what you will transition to. Is your next macrocycle going to be related to a different sport entirely? Do you want to focus on peaking in a different area of your current sport—for example, one that is related to speed instead of distance, or technique instead of power? Or do you want to repeat the same cycle and see what it feels like with increased intensities that translate into more power? It's up to you.

Microcycle

The *microcycle* represents one week in your program. In the sample meso-cycle we just discussed, the microcycle during the second phase might look like this:

- *Monday:* General conditioning; 45 minutes of light to moderate aerobic exercise, 30 minutes of general strength conditioning.
- *Tuesday and Thursday:* Sport-specific training; intervals to build short-term power, resistance exercises that target the specific muscles used in your sport.
- *Wednesday and Friday:* Technique drills.

Training Sessions

Depending on the frequency you're able to devote to your fitness routine, there are between three and six training sessions per microcycle (or week). Your training sessions should vary in intensity. Always follow a hard day with an easy one.

Training Units

Use the following elements to organize a training session (not every session will have all units):

- Warm-up: *every session*
- Flexibility: *every session*
- Aerobic conditioning: *selected sessions*
- Anaerobic (sprint, short-term endurance) conditioning: *selected sessions*

- Resistance exercises: *selected sessions*
- Technique (drills and "teardown" exercises, which allow you to practice and perfect safe and efficient movement): *selected sessions*
- Cool-down, with light stretching: *every session*

Using the skiing example, your first two weeks would be spent with general conditioning exercises to get your overall strength and endurance up. These would include light weightlifting, stretching, and aerobic work. The next two weeks would include sport-specific exercises that strengthen the muscles you'll be using when you ski.

During the next three weeks, you'll alternate the volume and intensity of your exercises between hard, moderate, and light workouts. Ideally, you should reduce the volume (not intensity) of your workouts and use the extra time to practice exercises that will contribute to your technique. Some health clubs have ski simulators that can help prepare you for your trip.

A week before your vacation, taper off. Once you get to your destination, you'll find you have the energy, strength, and fitness level that allow you to make the most of your time on the slopes. When you come back from your vacation, you can begin another macrocycle that focuses on another sport or simply on general fitness.

KJ CLOSEUP: Periodization

Periodization divides training into blocks of time known as *macrocycles, mesocycles,* and *microcycles*. It also identifies objectives, or training components, such as strength, endurance, technique, and even psychological factors. No matter what element or time frame you're dealing with in periodization, the principle is the same:

1. Break in slowly (adaptation)

2. Build in volume

3. Reduce volume and build in intensity

4. Reduce volume and intensity for the taper

5. Peak

6. Recover

Nutrition

You need adequate carbohydrates for energy, adequate protein to fight off infection and repair muscle tissue, and a minimal amount of fats to protect your organs. What you eat is as important as how much you eat. One study showed that subjects who reduced their fat consumption by half increased the nutritional value of their food as much as 50 percent, even though their total caloric intake dropped by 25 percent. Conversely, you can be malnourished even if your calorie consumption is high.

To calculate your calorie needs:

1. Determine your basal metabolic rate (BMR): This is the number of calories you would burn daily without any physical activity. Divide your body weight in pounds by 2.2 to get your weight in kilograms.

2. That's your BMR for one hour. Now multiply by 24 for your daily caloric expenditure when sedentary. If you weighed 180 pounds, it would work out like this:

$$180 \div 2.2 = 81.8$$
$$81.8 \times 24 = 1,963 \text{ calories}$$

3. Now adjust your BMR by gauging your activity level. Using the following scale, give yourself the allotted number of points for each entry. Afterward, you'll register a score.

Activity	Points
1. I usually walk to and from work or shopping (at least half a mile each way).	1
2. I usually take the stairs rather than using elevators or escalators.	1
3. The type of physical activity involved in my job or daily household routine is best described by the following statement (select only one of the next three):	
a. Most of my day is spent in office work, light physical activity, or household chores.	0
b. Most of my day is spent in farm activities, moderate physical activity, brisk walking, or comparable activities.	4

Activity	Points
c. My typical workday includes several hours of heavy physical activity (such as shoveling or lifting).	9
4. I do several hours of gardening or lawn work each week.	1
5. I fish once a week or more, on the average. (Fishing must involve active work such as rowing a boat. Dock sitting does not count.)	1
6. At least once a week, I participate for an hour or more in vigorous dancing like square dancing or folk dancing.	1
7. In season, I play golf at least once a week, and I do not use a power cart.	2
8. I often walk for exercise or recreation.	1
9. When I feel bothered by pressure at work or home, I use exercise as a way to relax.	1
10. Two or more times a week, I use calisthenic exercises (such as sit-ups or push-ups) for at least 10 minutes per session.	3
11. I regularly participate in yoga or perform stretching exercises.	2
12. I participate in active recreational sports such as tennis or handball (select only one of the next three):	
a. About once a week	2
b. About twice a week	4
c. Three times a week or more	7
13. I participate in vigorous fitness activities such as jogging or swimming at least 20 continuous minutes per session (select only one of the next three):	
a. About once a week	3
b. About twice a week	5
c. Three times a week or more	10

4. Add the points and check the chart below to find your score (1.0–1.9).

Points	Score	Description
0 to 1	1.0	Sedentary
2 to 10	1.3	Fairly inactive
11 to 20	1.5	Moderately active
21 to 30	1.7	Very active
31 to 40	1.9	Vigorously active

5. Now multiply your score by your BMR to find out how many calories your body requires each day for your particular activity level. For example, the range for our 180-pound male would be 1,963 calories if he were sedentary, and 3,730 calories if he were highly active.

Carbohydrates

Carbohydrates are your primary source of muscle energy. Complex carbohydrates such as breads, whole grains, and pastas get broken down into glucose—a pure form of nutritional energy—and then stored as glycogen in the liver and the muscles for use as fuel. Simple sugars such as fructose, dietary glucose, and processed flours and cereals don't need to be broken down, so they are absorbed more rapidly. The problem with this "quick energy" is that it tricks your body into thinking there is an ample supply of glucose steadily entering the bloodstream, when in fact it's just a short burst. The "sugar high" is a result of the bloodstream gathering up all the glucose. It's inevitably followed by a sugar low, since that glucose is short-lived and easily depleted. However, it is true that a lowfat candy bar or sports drink containing simple sugars can provide quick, useful energy if you take it immediately prior to exercise (ingesting fat prior to exercise can cause stomach upset).

Complex carbohydrates provide a more natural, even flow of energy. They make use of the body's innate processing abilities so that glucose is released gradually into the bloodstream. Glycogen can be replenished by the slow-burning complex carbohydrates on an ongoing basis.

Protein

Until 20 years ago, athletes' training tables were piled high with steaks, and protein was king. The reasoning was that since muscle tissue is made up of protein strands, eating more protein would build more muscle. In the 1960s, however, researchers established that protein doesn't fuel muscle—carbohydrates do. In fact, as a pre-event food, protein can diminish performance because it's difficult to digest and, when in the stomach, draws blood away from the working muscles.

Meats offer the most complete proteins—they have a full complement of the amino acids needed to create enzymes and hormones, fight off infection, help in the elimination of wastes, and build cell membranes. However, because most meats are high in saturated fats, and thus implicated in heart disease, your meat intake should be moderate. Other good sources of amino acids are milk, fish, and chicken, which also provide amino acid balance similar to our own tissue proteins. While plant sources contain amino acids as well, they tend to be deficient in tryptophan and lysine. Soybeans, beans, and other legumes are next in line; at the bottom are grains and cereals.

The U.S. government's recommendation for protein intake, which does not take into account level of activity, is .8 grams of protein per kilogram of body weight per day, or about 12 percent of your total calories. Once again, divide your body weight by 2.2 to get your weight in kilograms. For a 170-pound man, the formula looks like this:

$$170 \div 2.2 = 77.2 \text{ kg}$$
$$77.2 \text{ kg} \times 8 = 61.76 \text{ grams}$$

Each gram of protein has four calories, so that comes out to about 250 calories per day. You can get that from six ounces of meat, chicken, or fish, and two glasses of milk.

KJ TIP: Using More Protein by Eating Less Protein

To really ensure that your body uses more protein, make sure to get enough carbohydrate calories in your diet. When carbohydrate intake is insufficient, the body tends to convert higher amounts of protein into glucose for use as energy, which means less is available for repairing muscle tissue. By sticking to a diet that favors carbohydrates over proteins, you're allowing the body to use the protein for the purposes it was designed.

Fats

Because of its association with cardiovascular disease, your fat intake should comprise no more than 30 percent of your diet, and preferably closer to 10 percent. However, percentage isn't the only factor to consider; also important is the type of fat you consume. In France and Greece, where many rural-living people subsist on traditional diets that are as high as 45 percent in fat calories, studies have shown an extremely low incidence of heart disease. At first, perplexed researchers labeled this apparent contradiction the *French paradox*. However, it has since become clear that the fats consumed by these people are mostly derived from olive oil; they are *monounsaturated*, high in the antioxidant vitamin E, and apparently increase levels of HDL (the good cholesterol). By contrast, the American diet is high in *saturated* fats (so called because they are saturated with hydrogen atoms), which are derived from meats and are the most likely to lead to atherosclerosis (clogged arteries). How do you know if it's a saturated fat? If it solidifies at room temperature, like butter or shortening, it's saturated.

But the Mediterranean diet is also distinguished by other protective factors not common to the typical American diet:

- High consumption of fresh fruits and vegetables
- Low consumption of meats
- Moderately low consumption of dairy products
- Moderate consumption of alcohol, which also seems to increase HDL

Many research studies have confirmed the Mediterranean diet's superior benefits. In fact, a study of post–heart-attack patients placed on the Mediterranean diet found that they were 70 percent less likely to suffer from follow-up illness or death than patients who were placed on a highly fat-restricted diet.

Supplements

Americans spend about $3.3 billion annually on nutritional supplements in the form of packaged vitamins, minerals, and amino acids. Supplement use is highest among athletes who are, in almost all other respects, considered well-informed about health research. In the past five years alone, beta-hydroxy, beta-methylbutyrate, creatine phosphate, melatonin, chromium picolinate, and a range of other products have been touted as aids to building muscle, losing fat, and boosting energy.

But with few exceptions—none of which relate to otherwise healthy individuals—there's no evidence that these expensive products work. Studies have shown that athletes who take mineral and vitamin supplements for long periods of time fare no better than those who don't when both groups are eating an otherwise balanced, healthy diet.

Hydration

When you sweat during exercise, the fluid loss causes a reduction in plasma, the liquid medium of blood. As a result, your heart must work harder in order to circulate less blood and therefore less oxygen. It can affect your performance and even lead to collapse. The most extreme conditions for dehydration occur when you exercise in air that is hot and humid, because the sweat accumulates around your pores, making it harder for your body to regulate its internal temperature.

In order to avoid dehydration:

- Drink a glass of water within half an hour of exercise, or during your warm-up.
- Drink four to eight ounces of water for every 15 to 20 minutes of exercise, or every three to four miles of running.
- Drink plenty of fluids after exercise.
- In hot, humid weather, wear synthetic sports fabrics designed to wick moisture away from your body, leaving your pores open and cooling your body.

Sports Drinks

The main advantage of sports drinks and mixes is that they enhance the flavor of water and thus encourage you to drink adequate amounts of fluid. The nutritional value of sports drinks is another matter; many of them do contain small amounts of *electrolytes* (potassium and sodium). However, if you're otherwise healthy, it's unlikely that you would need to have electrolytes replenished, even after a long and grueling workout.

Many sports drinks also contain carbohydrates in the form of simple sugars, such as sucrose and fructose. These may provide some quick energy. However, your main concern when exercising is dehydration, not nutrition; and since carbohydrates will slow the absorption of water from your stomach, sports drinks are not advisable during a workout. As for postexercise replenishment, sports drinks are fine.

Sports drinks that contain protein or amino acids have no proved benefits; taken before or during exercise, they may cause stomach upset.

Exercising at High Altitude

Higher altitudes have a lower volume of oxygen available in the air, which means your body must work much harder to supply itself with fuel. Even an altitude change of 2,000 feet above the level you're normally used to can bring with it such symptoms as fatigue, breathlessness, a small increase in heart rate, and headaches. When you go on ski or snowboard vacations or camping trips at elevation, give yourself a day or two to acclimate; keep your activity level moderate; drink plenty of water; and avoid fatty foods, alcoholic beverages, and cigarettes, all of which can further interfere with your body's ability to absorb oxygen. When you're ready to hit the slopes or trails, go with a partner, and pay attention to signs of fatigue. Advanced altitude sickness—which is rare under 8,000 feet—includes disorientation, severe breathlessness, hallucinations, and coughing up blood.

Cold-Weather Sports

The growing popularity of cold-weather sports makes it easy to stay fit and active in the winter, but there are some special concerns for playing in the outdoors:

- In order to maintain its internal thermostat, your body has to work harder in cold weather, which means your heart rate will be higher and you'll fatigue more rapidly—so adjust your level of exercise accordingly.
- Dress properly. Efficient temperature control depends on keeping moisture away from your body, something for which cotton is poorly suited. Wool, wool blends, and weather-conscious synthetic materials such as Capilene and polypropylene are better choices. For stop-start activities like skiing or snowboarding, use a layering system that allows you to shed or bundle up, depending on your level of activity at any particular time. The layers should include an inner layer to wick away the moisture produced by your body; an insulating middle layer such as fleece, to protect you from wind and cold; and an outer shell layered with Gore-Tex or some other wind and waterproof material, to keep the outside moisture from coming in. Several extreme-weather gear apparel

companies make staying warm and comfortable easy with multilayer product lines.

- Beware of frostbite. *Frostbite* occurs in stages; the first sign, known as *frostnip*, causes the skin to turn white and waxy. The most common sites are the fingers and toes. Frostnip is reversible if you get out of the cold and soak the affected area in warm water. In advanced stages of frostbite, however, circulation in the extremities begins to shut down, and that brings with it the risk of permanent damage to the affected areas. Once cold penetrates beneath the skin, it begins to affect the core of your body, a condition known as *hypothermia*; death can result within a couple of hours.

- Fluid loss increases with your activity level, even in cold temperatures. Make sure to drink plenty of water throughout the day.

Coping with Pain

For the average individual, the benefits of lifelong physical activity far outweigh the risks. However, it's inevitable that at some point, you will need to manage some type of a minor, nagging pain. There are several options.

Over-the-Counter Medications

There are three categories of over-the-counter (OTC) drugs commonly used for the treatment of pain: aspirin, acetaminophen (Tylenol), and ibuprofen (Advil). All three provide pain relief, but only aspirin and ibuprofen reduce inflammation as well (they are NSAIDs), thus actually speeding the healing process. Aspirin, however, is more likely to cause stomach upset. If aspirin or ibuprofen is being used for its anti-inflammatory effect, you need to build up a certain level of the drug in your system and then maintain it in order for it to work as an anti-inflammatory. If this is the desired effect, you must take the drug as instructed on the bottle, not just when the pain is acute. If you have any doubts, questions, or concerns, consult your physician first.

With severe ruptures and contusions, avoid anti-inflammatory drugs for the first 48 hours, unless otherwise directed by your doctor. During the initial stages, the drugs can actually increase bleeding by reducing the blood's ability to clot. If you're in doubt about the nature or extent of your injury, take acetaminophen only, and consult your physician.

KJ TIP: Be Careful with OTC Painkillers

There is no such thing as a safe drug, even one that's available over-the-counter. To avoid complications:

• Always follow package recommendations.

• Avoid alcohol.

• If you're taking any other medications—OTC or not—consult your physician first.

• If you experience any adverse effects, stop taking the medication and consult your physician.

Corticosteroids

Corticosteroids can only be administered by a physician. They can dramatically decrease inflammation, and in some cases, such as bursitis, may resolve the condition completely. These drugs are potentially dangerous, though, so they are only occasionally used. If overused, they can actually weaken the tissue, leading to further injury. (Do not confuse corticosteroids with *anabolic steroids*, the synthetic testosterone compounds that some athletes use to enhance performance, in spite of their dangerous side effects and the fact that their use is banned in most competitions.)

Transcutaneous Electrical Neural Stimulation (TENS)

Portable TENS devices, worn on the hip like a personal stereo, administer electrical signals to the injured area that block the transmission of the pain message to the brain. These devices are sometimes incorporated into rehabilitation therapy.

Ice

Ice is an excellent remedy for pain and inflammation. It increases blood flow to the injured area by initially slowing blood flow and constricting the blood vessels; your brain then perceives that area of the body as cold and sends more blood there to warm it up. Ice has the added benefit of numbing the area, therefore decreasing pain. Always place a towel between your skin and the ice to minimize the possibility of frostbite; keep the pack on for 5 to 15 minutes and apply two or three times a day. Some companies manufacture elastic compression pads that include an enclosure for an ice packet. Even a bag of frozen vegetables such as peas or corn can be used, as it molds well to the injured area.

Heat

Heat also increases blood flow. It does so by opening up (dilating) the blood vessels. It should not be used in the first 48 hours following an injury, as the dilation of the blood vessels can increase the active bleeding in the area. Heat can be applied in the form of an electrical heating pad, a hot bath, or a warm towel. If you're using range-of-motion exercises to rehabilitate an injured limb, precede the exercises with 15 to 20 minutes of heat, which relaxes and loosens the muscles and tendons.

Alternating Ice and Heat

Alternating ice and heat as part of rehabilitation therapy cycles fluids through an injured area. The ice reduces the swelling and clears the area of fluids that have been sitting around in the affected joint or limb. The heat reintroduces fresh blood to help speed healing. You can alternate ice and heat at home using one bucket filled with ice, and one filled with warm water. Immersion is effective because it bathes the entire joint and allows for movement while the joint is submerged. Alternate between the two for a 15- to 20-minute period.

Ultrasound

An ultrasound device sends high-frequency sound waves beneath the surface of the skin. The sound waves make the molecules of the tissue bounce around, generating a deep heat and increasing circulation in the process. Ultrasound may also be helpful in influencing the scar tissue that forms in the healing process to align with the muscle and tendon tissue.

Acupuncture

Recent studies have demonstrated acupuncture to be beneficial in reducing certain types of pain, though it's not clear how long-lasting these effects are.

Massage

Many forms of massage are now available for the treatment of sports injuries. Of particular relevance for sports injuries are neuromuscular, deep tissue, and sports massage, all of which concentrate on specific areas of muscle, increasing circulation and relieving scarring, adhesions, and trigger points by applying firm pressure against the grain of the muscle fibers.

18

A Final Word

What's the single most important organ when it comes to sports and fitness? Without a question, it's the brain. What happens between your ears makes all the difference in such areas as enjoyment, motivation, judgment, and choice. These are the factors that will ultimately determine which activities you choose, how you pursue them, and how long you stick with them. If knowledge and ability were enough, then many more Americans—and certainly many of our great ex-athletes—would maintain a program of lifetime fitness. Indeed, there have been several studies showing that getting people to exercise—even when their lives depend on it—is an enormously difficult, and often futile, undertaking.

Unfortunately, very few studies have attempted to explain why some people enthusiastically remain committed to a lifetime program of sports, fitness, and exercise, while others—the vast majority of others—either go through occasional bursts of activity and then lose interest, or opt for an altogether sedentary lifestyle. What *is* known is that the number-one reason most Americans give for inactivity is "lack of time," an excuse that, at least on the surface, doesn't mesh with the vast numbers of hours we spend watching television. (According to one study, the average American watches 15 hours of television a week, yet less than 22 percent of Americans exercise 60 minutes a week.)

The second most common reason cited for lack of activity is "concerns about health." This excuse has a certain irony since exercise, when done properly, can in fact help prevent or minimize nearly every conceivable type of health concern, ranging from back complaints to heart disease.

Why, really, are Americans so inactive? The most likely explanation is simply that we can be. We live in a world where people use motorized transportation to go even small distances, and perform jobs that involve sitting down all day. Nevertheless, some individuals seem to buck the overwhelming odds. Such people, regardless of their occupations, financial situations, or family commitments, have managed to make sports and exercise as routine as eating three meals a day. And you can, too.

The following seven recommendations comprise the final and perhaps most essential pieces of information you need to stay athletic forever:

1. *Maintain an awareness of the benefits of exercise, both short-term and long-term:* These benefits have been outlined in detail throughout this book. The top two reasons cited by most Americans for why they don't exercise—lack of time and health concerns—both reveal a lack of understanding about how important and beneficial physical activity is for everyone.

2. *Have confidence in your ability to participate in sports and exercise:* According to sport sociologists and psychologists, many adults don't explore their athletic potentials because of fear about how they might appear to others. Men traditionally do not participate in things they feel will make them look bad. If you were unathletic as a child, or if you limited yourself to only one sport, you may have unconsciously opted out of activities that you may actually enjoy now as an adult.

3. *Enjoy low- to moderate-intensity physical activity:* Ask any coach, trainer, or sports doctor the number-one reason why enthusiastic, active adults drop out of sports and exercise, and you will hear one answer: overdoing it. Low- to moderate-intensity exercise may be the most essential and undervalued element for long-term fitness and performance.

4. *Set goals and choose objectives:* Goals will—and should—change periodically to keep you interested, but always have a goal in mind. Perhaps it's weight loss; maybe you want to become a better runner; or

perhaps you've decided to take up a brand new sport. Knowing why you're exercising is key to staying motivated.

5. *Have role models:* It helps to be involved with people who are interested in the activities you're interested in—or to share your passion with friends and family who aren't. A good coach, mentor, or trainer is also important. Treat yourself to an occasional session with someone who can help you improve your athletic ability.

6. *Choose activities that are easy to access:* If you don't have easy access to the activities you're interested in—for example, a pool for swimming, trails for hiking, or slopes for skiing—then your participation will be limited. Come up with alternate activities you can do on a frequent basis.

7. *Cut back on your sedentary activities:* Television remains the biggest gobbler of American leisure time; it flickers for seven hours a day in the average American household. Pull the plug and go outside.

Finally, always enjoy yourself. While the world aspires to make everything from cooking to transportation convenient, fast, and automatic, your body's inclinations are and always will be, much more primal. To remain athletic forever you simply have to honor your body by engaging in the one thing it was designed for: movement. Move, and your body will faithfully adapt.

Glossary

Abductors   Muscles that move your arms or legs away from the center-line of your body (as when raising your arm or leg to the side).

Achilles tendon   Connects the calf muscles of the posterior lower leg to the heel bone.

ACL   *See* **Anterior cruciate ligament.**

Acromion process   A bony projection of the scapula that forms the tip of the shoulder.

Active rest   Light exercises that maintain fitness while allowing the body to recover from a hard workout.

Adductors   Muscles that move limbs inward, toward the centerline of the body.

Adenosine triphosphate–phosphocreatine (**ATP-PC**)   A fuel source that can provide the energy for muscle contractions during intense activities of short duration.

Adhesive capsulitis   A condition that causes the capsule of a joint to become stiff and immobile.

Aerobic activity   Continuous, rhythmic movement involving the large muscle groups functioning at an intensity level that elicits cardiovascular benefits.

Anaerobic glycolysis   An energy-producing system (that does not use oxygen) used by the body when the activity is of intense but brief duration.

Anaerobic threshold   The point at which the body shifts energy systems from aerobic (requiring oxygen) to anaerobic (not requiring oxygen).

Anterior cruciate ligament (ACL)   A ligament that attaches the femur (thigh bone) to the tibia (leg bone), giving the knee stability.

Articulations   Joints.

ATP-PC   *See* **Adenosine triphosphate–phosphocreatine.**

Basal metabolic rate (BMR)   An individual's expenditure of energy when he or she is at rest.

Biarticular muscle   A muscle that crosses two joints.

Biceps   The anterior, upper arm muscles located at the shoulder and elbow.

Biceps femoris   One of the hamstring muscles located in the posterior thigh.

Black toe   An injury usually caused by repeated trauma to the toe that results in bleeding under the toenail.

Blood volume   Amount of blood circulating through the body.

BMR   *See* **Basal metabolic rate.**

Bow wave   The pocket of air below the chin created as you roll your body to the side to breathe when swimming.

Bradycardia   Extremely slow heart rate.

Bursae   Fluid-filled sacs that minimize friction between bones and soft tissue.

Bursitis   Inflammation of a bursa.

Calcaneofibular ligament   A ligament that attaches the fibula (lateral leg bone) to the calcaneus, stabilizing the lateral ankle.

Calcaneus   Heel bone.

Capitellum   The portion of the humerus (upper arm bone) that articulates with the radius (forearm bone) to form one of the elbow joints.

Cardiac output   The amount of blood circulated by the heart per minute.

Carpal tunnel syndrome   An injury from overuse of the wrist; it causes inflammation in the area of a nerve that passes through the wrist, resulting in pain and/or numbness.

Carpals   Small bones that comprise the wrist.

Cervical spine   The upper third of the spinal column.

Chondrocytes   Specialized cartilage cells.

Chondromalacia patella   A softening of the cartilage behind the kneecap that can result in knee pain.

Chronic fatigue syndrome   A condition sometimes associated with overtraining.

Clavicle   The collarbone.

Coccyx   The tailbone.

Collateral vessels   Blood vessels created by intense exercise that allow more blood flow to the heart.

Compartment syndrome   An abnormal increase in pressure within a muscular compartment, usually in the lower leg, that can cause pain or numbness.

Concentric   A muscle contraction that occurs when a muscle shortens to overcome resistance (commonly when a weight is lifted).

Condyloid   A type of joint designed for both stability and range of motion.

Connective tissue   Specialized tissue with varying qualities of strength and resilience.

Contusion   An injury caused by a direct blow, resulting in bleeding within a muscle.

Corticosteroids   Synthetic hormones that can dramatically reduce inflammation.

Cranking   Bicycle pedaling against high resistance.

Damping   The shock absorption quality of athletic shoes.

Deltoid   Tri-part shoulder muscle.

Deltoid ligament   A triangular-shaped ligament on the medial part of the ankle.

Diastolic pressure   A reading of arterial pressure between heartbeats.

Dorsiflexion   Movement of the ankle in which the foot is raised upward toward the lower leg.

Eccentric   A muscle contraction that occurs when a muscle lengthens as resistance is applied (usually when a weight is being lowered).

Epicondylitis   Inflammation localized to the attachments of the wrist muscles at the inside or outside of the elbow.

Erector spinae   Muscles of the back contributing to movement and stability of the spine.

Facet joint syndrome   Back pain caused by degeneration of the articular cartilage of the joints that connect vertebrae.

Facet joints   Joints that are formed where two adjacent vertabrae are in contact with each other.

Familial hypercholesteremia   High cholesterol associated with a gene.

Fartlek   Spontaneous sprints incorporated into a light or moderate aerobic workout.

Fast-twitch (glycolytic) fibers   Muscle fibers associated with short-duration, high-intensity muscular contractions.

Femur   Thighbone.

Gastrocnemius   The primary calf muscle.

General adaptation syndrome   The mode by which one's body responds to stress.

Glenohumeral joint   One of the four joints of the shoulder.

Glenoid labrum   Fibrocartilage in the socket of the shoulder joint that functions to increase stability in the shoulder.

Golgi tendon organs   Sense organs that signal muscles to relax if too much resistance is experienced.

Hamstrings   The muscle complex at the rear of the thigh extending from the hip to the knee.

Heel spur   A bone deposit that forms at the attachment of the plantar fascia on the undersurface of the heel.

Hematoma   Pooling of blood in muscle tissue.

Herniated disc   A protrusion of the intervertebral disc that may impinge a nerve root and cause pain.

Humeroradial joint   One of the joints formed at the elbow.

Humeroulnar joint   One of the joints formed at the elbow.

Humerus   Upper arm bone.

Hyaline (articular) cartilage   Smooth cartilage that coats the ends of bones.

Hydrostatic weighing   A method of determining body fat composition by weighing a person underwater.

Hypertension   High blood pressure.

Hypertrophy   Muscle growth stimulated by exercise.

Hypokineticism   Lack of movement or exercise.

Iliotibial band   A long, thin band of tissue that runs laterally along the thigh from the hip to the knee.

Iliotibial band friction syndrome   Inflammation of the iliotibial band common in runners and cyclists.

Infraspinatus   One of the rotator cuff muscles.

Intervertebral discs   A pad of fibrocartilage that sits between vertebrae of the spine.

Inversion sprain   The most common type of ankle sprain in which the foot twists inward, injuring the lateral ligaments of the ankle.

Isokinetic training   A form of exercise in which speed is held constant and resistance is regulated throughout the range of motion.

Isometric training   Resistance exercises in which a muscle is contracted without movement of the associated joint.

Isotonic training   Strength training involving a fixed amount of weight.

Joint capsule   A fibrous capsule enveloping a joint.

Joint receptors   Structures that provide information to the brain about the position of a joint.

Karvonen method   A method of gauging exercise intensity.

Lactic acid system   *See* **Anaerobic glycolysis**.

Lumbar spine   The lower third of the spine.

Maladaptation   Negative effects, including injuries caused by overtraining.

Maximum aerobic capacity ($\dot{V}O_2$max)   The point at which oxygen uptake by the body fails to increase with an intensified workload.

Menisci   Fibrocartilage discs that reduce the compressive forces within a joint, especially the knee.

Motor units   A collection of muscle fibers stimulated by one nerve.

Myositis ossificans   A bony deposit that forms within a muscle when the muscle is injured from a forceful impact.

Nucleus pulposus   Semifluid material in the central portion of the intervertebral discs.

Olecranon   The bony tip of elbow.

Orthotics   Shoe inserts that can improve the biomechanics of the foot.

Osteochondritis   Injury to the articular cartilage that may cause a fragment to break loose and float into the joint, interfering with normal motion.

Osteoporosis of disuse   Weakening of the bone from lack of movement.

Overtraining   Exercise beyond the point at which the body is able to adapt positively.

Overuse syndrome   Injuries such as strains or stress fractures that occur when a joint or limb is overused.

Paresthesia   Numbness.

Patellofemoral pain syndrome   Anterior knee pain that can arise from a variety of activities.

Periodization   A calendar approach to sports training popular among elite athletes.

Periosteum   Thin lining of bone tissue.

Pes cavus   High arches.

Pes planus   Flat feet.

Phalanges   Small bones of the fingers and toes.

Plantar fascia   Arch ligament of the foot.

Plantar fascitis   Inflammation of the arch ligament.

Plantarflexion   Movement of the ankle in which the foot is pushed downward.

Point tenderness   A sign of injury in which localized pain is felt when pressure is applied to a specific area.

Popliteal fossa   The area behind the knee joint.

Posterior cruciate ligament   A stabilizing ligament of the knee that attaches the femur to the tibia.

Progressive resistance overload   The primary principle of strength training whereby the load is gradually increased, resulting in adaptations in the muscle that increase its strength.

Pronation   Rolling of the arch of the foot toward the ground.

Proprioceptors   Organ units that relay information to the brain about body position and movement.

Push-up plus   A normal push-up supplemented with an additional extension of the shoulders at the point of maximum contraction.

Quadriceps tendon   The broad tendon that connects the quadriceps muscles to the top of the patella.

Radius   One of the two forearm bones.

Rectus femoris   A quadriceps muscle.

Rotator cuff   A complex of muscles and tendons responsible for stabilizing the shoulder throughout its range of motion.

Sciatica   Radiating pain in the lower extremity caused by pressure on a nerve in the lumbar spine.

Sequestrated disc A condition in which a fragment of the interverte-bral disc comes loose.

Sesamoiditis Inflammation of the sesamoid bones at the ball of the foot.

Skinfold testing A simple method for determining body fat composi-tion using calipers.

Sliding filaments theory A proposed theory of muscular movement that asserts muscle fibers contract in a telescoping fashion.

Slow-twitch (oxidative) fibers Muscle fibers adapted for long-term, moderate-intensity contractions, such as standing, walking, or light jogging.

Spondylolisthesis Forward slippage of a vertebra relative to the verte-bra below it.

Spondylosis A misshapen vertebra either from a congenital defect or from an injury.

Sprain Stretching or tearing of a ligament.

Strain Stretching or tearing of muscle-tendon fibers.

Stress fracture Damaging small cracks in the bone resulting from overuse.

Stroke volume The amount of blood pumped by the heart per beat.

Supination Outward rolling of the foot during normal striding movements.

Supraspinatus A rotator cuff muscle.

Syndesmosis The area joining the two bones of the lower leg where they meet just above the ankle.

Synovial fluid The body's natural joint lubricant.

Systolic pressure The pressure of blood against the arterial walls when the heart is in midbeat.

Taper   A temporary reduction in training volume that may allow the body to recover and therefore improve one's performance.

Target heart rate   An established goal for exercise intensity measured by the number of heartbeats per minute.

Tendinitis   Inflammation of a tendon.

Thoracic spine   The middle third of the spinal column.

Training effect   Positive changes elicited by exercise stress.

Trochanteric   Relating to a bony protrusion of the femur near the hip.

Turf toe   Inflammation, pain, and stiffness of the big toe.

Ulna   One of the two forearm bones.

Ulnar nerve impingement   Irritation of the nerve that runs along the inner aspect of the elbow; it can cause a tingling pain in that area.

Valsalva maneuver   Temporary pressure buildup in an enclosed cavity of the body.

Vastus medialis oblique   One of the quadriceps muscles in the front of the thigh.

White coat hypertension   A temporary spike in blood pressure caused by the anxiety one may feel when visiting a physician; it can cause a false blood-pressure reading.

Index